CONSTITUTIONAL AGENCY

CLARENDON LAW LECTURES SERIES

War
ANDREW CLAPHAM

Natural Law and Natural Rights (2nd edition)
JOHN FINNIS

Land Law (3rd edition)
ELIZABETH COOKE

Employment Law (2nd edition)
HUGH COLLINS

Competition Law and Antitrust
DAVID J. GERBER

International Law
VAUGHAN LOWE

Introduction to Company Law (3rd edition)
PAUL DAVIES

Civil Liberties
CONOR GEARTY

The Conflict of Laws (4th edition)
ADRIAN BRIGGS

Intellectual Property
MICHAEL SPENCE

Bentham and the Common Law Tradition (2nd edition)
GERALD POSTEMA

Policies and Perceptions of Insurance Law in the Twenty-First Century (2nd edition)
MALCOLM CLARKE

Law and Values in the European Union
STEPHEN WEATHERILL

Philosophy of Private Law
WILLIAM LUCY

Personal Property Law (4th edition)
MICHAEL BRIDGE

Law in Modern Society
DENIS GALLIGAN

The Idea of Arbitration
JAN PAULSSON

An Introduction to Tort Law (2nd edition)
TONY WEIR

The Anthropology of Law
FERNANDA PIRIE

Equity (2nd edition)
SARAH WORTHINGTON

Law and Gender
JOANNE CONAGHAN

Atiyah's Introduction to the Law of Contract (6th edition)
STEPHEN A. SMITH AND P. S. ATIYAH

The Concept of Law (3rd edition)
H.L.A. HART

With a Postscript edited by Penelope A. Bulloch and Joseph Raz With an Introduction and Notes by Leslie Green

Unjust Enrichment (2nd edition)
PETER BIRKS

Land Law (2nd Edition)
ELIZABETH COOKE

An Introduction to Family Law (2nd edition)
GILLIAN DOUGLAS

Administrative Law (5th edition)
PETER CANE

Criminal Justice
LUCIA ZEDNER

Discrimination Law (2nd edition)
SANDRA FREDMAN

Contract Theory
STEPHEN A. SMITH

An Introduction to the Law of Trusts (3rd edition)
SIMON GARDNER

CONSTITUTIONAL AGENCY

PHILIP SALES

OXFORD
UNIVERSITY PRESS

OXFORD
UNIVERSITY PRESS

Great Clarendon Street, Oxford, OX2 6DP,
United Kingdom

Oxford University Press is a department of the University of Oxford.
It furthers the University's objective of excellence in research, scholarship,
and education by publishing worldwide. Oxford is a registered trade mark of
Oxford University Press in the UK and in certain other countries.

Published in the United States of America by Oxford University Press
546 Fifth Avenue, New York, NY 10036, United States of America

British Library Cataloguing in Publication Data
Data available

Library of Congress Control Number: 2026946687

ISBN 978–0–19–792837–0

DOI: 10.1093/oso/9780197928370.001.0001

The manufacturer's authorized representative in the EU for product safety is
Oxford University Press España S.A. of Parque Empresarial San Fernando de Henares,
Avenida de Castilla, 2 – 28830 Madrid (www.oup.es/en or product.safety@oup.com).
OUP España S.A. also acts as importer into Spain of products made by the manufacturer.

For Miranda

Acknowledgements

Several people provided me with very helpful comments when the lectures were delivered. In particular, I would like to thank Jonathan Morgan, Harshan Kumarasingham, Tarun Khaitan, Timothy Endicott, Richard Ekins, Nick Barber and the anonymous reviewers for OUP. Very kindly, Richard and Nick also read through the manuscript of the book and made detailed comments on it, as did Monty Fynn and Sir Jack Beatson. I am very grateful to them all.

Contents

Table of Cases

Table of Legislation

Table of European Materials

I

Introduction

Right without might is helpless, might without right is tyrannical (Pascal, *Pensées*)

It is a great folly to want to be wise on your own (La Rochefoucauld, *Collected Maxims*)

The title for this book and the Clarendon lectures 2025 on which it is based is deliberately ambiguous. I want to look at the constitutional agency of the executive, the legislature and the courts. My focus is on the UK institutions, rather than the devolved institutions.

What does 'constitutional agency' mean? It has a double aspect. On the one hand, I propose to examine the agency that the constitution creates for each of these institutions in giving them the capacity to act. On the other, I propose to examine the agency they have in terms of being able by their actions to modify the constitution itself.

What does it mean to talk about the constitution in the context of the law of the UK, focusing in particular on the law of England and Wales?

The UK does not have a single comprehensive constitutional document which can act as the reference point to identify constitutional issues. I am not seeking to use the term 'constitutional' in that sort of precise way, but rather to indicate an area of law and political practice where decisions are made which are of particular prominence and importance for the allocation of decision-making authority in relation to the exercise of public power, as between executive, legislature and courts. In this sense, constitutional law shades into ordinary administrative law. Also, there are areas of

Constitutional Agency. Philip Sales, Oxford University Press. © Philip Sales 2026.
DOI: 10.1093/oso/9780197928370.003.0001

constitutional law and practice which exist but only rarely come before the courts.

Gillian Peele provides a schema for assessing constitutions.[1] She points to the importance of political culture in their operation—'the complex set of values, attitudes and assumptions, political prejudices and practices that interact with the more formal elements of a constitutional system'.[2] Political culture is particularly important in the case of the UK, in view of its lack of a comprehensive written constitutional document and, in consequence, a certain lack of clear positive rules of constitutional *law*. The principal points Peele emphasises about political culture are the extent of consensus within the polity, the role of the judiciary and the modes of legal argument, the character of constitutional argument, attitudes towards the state, the attitude of the media and procedures for constitutional change. She observes that:

> the particular mix of modes of argument which will command legitimacy is not something which . . . is cut and dried or can be nicely measured. It reflects the nuances of a legal culture and the varying weight placed on such values as equality, procedural justice and fairness as well as broad assumptions of social policy. The fact that a court may appeal to a variety of values in the wider society and that the particular mix that will give it legitimacy may change with the passage of time is then one which makes it necessary to look beyond formal legal doctrines for an understanding of how courts interact with the polity.[3]

The state is dependent on the support of those subject to it. It needs to exercise power in a way which meets what Bernard Williams called the basic legitimation demand.[4] Sources of legitimacy are varied and may fluctuate and change as circumstances and the expectations and the

1 G. Peele, 'Comparing Constitutions', ch 10 in D. Kavanagh and G. Peele (eds), *Comparative Government and Politics: Essays in Honour of S.E. Finer* (1984).

2 Ibid, 196–197.

3 Ibid, 203.

4 B. Williams, *In the Beginning was the Deed: Realism and Moralism in Political Argument* (2005), 3–6. The basic legitimation demand is that the state should answer the fundamental political question, namely how 'order, protection, safety, trust and the conditions of cooperation' are to be secured, by being able to hold itself out to its subjects as the legitimate source of governance.

demands of citizens change in response. Giving citizens voice through democratic processes and the ability to enforce their rights in court may be an important basis for securing legitimacy for the state and its laws.

The UK is aptly described as a liberal democracy. The liberal element refers to the liberty and autonomy which the political order seeks to achieve for individuals. The democratic element refers to self-government and collective autonomy. The liberal element is the area of protection by individual rights under the rule of law. The democratic element relates to law-making in Parliament, the area protected by the principle of the sovereignty of Parliament. At the heart of the UK constitution is the tension between these two elements. One of the principal objects of the constitution is to achieve their stable, reasonable and acceptable integration. But it also needs to secure a state which has the authority to act and is effective in acting. That is the area where the executive needs to have agency.

Describing the UK as a liberal democracy is to use modern terminology. But the roots of the UK constitution in ideas of this type go far back in history. To use different and older terminology, the guiding principles of the UK's constitution are freedom and responsible government. The UK's political-legal governance system has revolved around these ideas since well before the development in the nineteenth and twentieth centuries of democratic ideology as a dominant legitimating concept for government.[5] In a period when it is sometimes said that democracy itself is under threat, it is perhaps significant to recall this. Freedom and responsible government are valuable and have long been treated as such in the UK's constitutional order.

Freedom under the law recognises the value of and protects individual autonomy, promoting the basic ability of individuals to form their own opinions and to live their lives according to those opinions. Responsible government aims to ensure the accountability of rulers to those whose interests they represent in governing. This is direct accountability to Parliament itself, including by the requirement for a Prime Minister to be

5 J. Dunn (ed), *Democracy: the Unfinished Journey 508 BC to AD 1993* (1992); J. Dunn, *Setting the People Free: The Story of Democracy* (2005); F. Fukuyama, *The End of History and the Last Man* (1992).

able to command the confidence of a majority in the House of Commons;[6] and also accountability to the electorate, by reason of the need for rulers to seek re-election periodically. Parliament developed in the period before the twentieth century as a body that was representative in various ways, particularly by reference to locality through the representation of boroughs and shires. This was before it was democratic in terms of a general franchise for all citizens. This pattern of government proved to be eminently adaptable to accommodate democratic ideology, as that grew in importance. Hence we have arrived at what is described now as a liberal democracy.

The words 'liberal' and 'democracy' have acquired connotations in certain contexts which can be regarded as negative. 'Liberal' in American political parlance has a meaning very different from that which tends to be given to it in Europe. In American usage it carries a meaning which presupposes substantive political positions to a far greater extent than is the case in Europe. 'Democracy' is also an ambiguous word with a contested meaning. There are different forms of democracy (such as direct, representative, deliberative etc.), with different political implications. Autocratic regimes often claim to have democratic endorsement to legitimise themselves through elections, which may be rigged.

We should not be misled by language so as to overlook the older principles underlying the UK's constitution. It is a constitution founded on freedom under the law and responsible government. Under modern conditions these principles mean that it is also a constitution based on the rule of law and representative democracy.

These are ideas which have substantive moral content. They are not neutral concepts compatible with *any* form of political regime. Any constitution by which a nation is to govern itself requires a basic commitment to certain values. Freedom under the law and responsible government are the fundamental values of our constitution. They are values or principles stated at a fairly general level, and there is scope for a good deal of debate and argument about how they should be worked through

6 For an account of the origins of this after the Glorious Revolution of 1688, see G. Owers, *The Rage of Party: How Whig Versus Tory Made Modern Britain* (2025).

in detail. But they provide the basic orientation for the constitutional enterprise in the UK. They have normative substance and impose normative requirements. It is a separate question how those normative requirements should be met, whether by enforcement of them as legal rules or through political custom and practice.

This view of the foundational commitments of the constitution has implications regarding the boundary between law and political custom and practice as regulatory mechanisms. The closer one comes to the centre of each of these values, of individual freedom and responsible government, the greater the normative force which it generates, and the stronger the case for interpreting the applicable principle as one of law rather than mere convention.

This is true of the principle of responsible government: the doctrine of parliamentary sovereignty is a legal rule applicable where Parliament itself, as the representative democratic body, legislates. The courts enforce primary legislation as binding law by application of this legal rule. They do not leave the application of statutes to be treated as a matter of political convention, which might be departed from. It is also true of the value of freedom under the law. This has effects in positive law, for example in relation to statutory interpretation (in particular, by application of the 'principle of legality', discussed later in this book, so as to minimise the impact of statute on fundamental rights so far as possible[7]) and in terms of the application of the rationality standard in public law, where heightened scrutiny (or so-called 'anxious scrutiny') may be applicable where fundamental rights are interfered with.[8] The two values may come into conflict, in which case the relationship between them also has to be mediated by the law. Hence it is established that the principle of legality only gives rise to a legal presumption, which means that Parliament can override it if it uses clear statutory language to do so.

7 See *R v Secretary of State for the Home Department, ex p Simms* [2000] 2 AC 115, 131 (per Lord Hoffmann: 'Fundamental rights cannot be overridden by general or ambiguous words [in a statute]').

8 See *ex p Simms* [2000] 1 AC 115, 130 (per Lord Steyn: 'the more substantial the interference with fundamental rights the more the court will require by way of justification before it can be satisfied that the interference is reasonable in a public law sense').

The conceptual foundations of this book and the series of lectures on which it is based are located in the work of Montesquieu, Albert Venn Dicey and Frederic Maitland. My debt to Maitland will be obvious at various points. From Montesquieu I take the idea that the British constitution is to be characterised as a constitution of freedom. This was indeed what made it so attractive to him and to continental writers in the eighteenth century. For Montesquieu, what made the British constitution one in which political freedom was achieved was what he saw as the separation of powers according to the basic tripartite division of the constitutional order into the executive, the legislature and the courts.[9] This division has provided a helpful general organising framework which has stood the test of time, capable of accommodating the different legitimation needs of a modern liberal democratic state: namely, respect for the democratic principle (the legislature), respect for a principle of effective state action (the executive) and respect for the principle of the rule of law (the courts). Although that division was inaccurate as a description of Britain's polity at the time Montesquieu was writing and remains so to some degree, it maps out distinct paradigm functions of the modern state and has proved remarkably resilient.

Dicey's account of the UK's constitutional law in his *Introduction to the Study of the Law of the Constitution*[10] has also been extensively criticised and cannot be supported in all its details. But in its essentials it has also proved remarkably resilient. I contend that it continues to provide us with important insights into the structure and operation of the UK's constitution.

Dicey's identification of parliamentary sovereignty and the rule of law as the two fundamental pillars of the constitution maps onto the basic features of the UK as a liberal democratic polity, seeking to give effect to the principle of collective self-government and the principle of individual liberty. The third part of his book is concerned with conventions as a third pillar of the constitution, the aspect of the British constitution

9 Montesquieu, *The Spirit of the Laws* (1748), Book 11, chapter 6; Book 19, chapter 27.
10 A.V. Dicey, *Introduction to the Study of the Law of the Constitution* 8th ed (1915).

concerning 'constitutional or political ethics',[11] as distinct from legal rules enforceable by the courts. In the late nineteenth and early twentieth centuries, the political morality element of the constitution was thick and broadly effective as a constraint on the exercise of power. As Nevil Johnson explains: 'The efficient secret of the constitution lay in the fact that through its institutions and practices it expressed a capacity held to be inherent in the society and its ruling elites to make those institutions work, to devise practical solutions to the problems of governing in a rapidly changing society and an expanding overseas empire, and to give stability to the future by sustaining habits and conventions of civilised social and political life.'[12] Gladstone wrote that the British constitution 'presumes more boldly than any other, the good sense and the good faith of those who work it'.[13] He went on:

> If, unhappily, these personages meet together, on the great area of a nation's fortunes, as jockeys meet upon a racecourse, each to urge to the uttermost, as against the others, the power of the animal he rides; or as counsel in a court, each to procure the victory of his client, without respect to any other interest or right: then this boasted Constitution of ours is neither more nor less than a heap of absurdities. The undoubted competency of each reaches even to the paralysis or destruction of the rest.[14]

It is significant that he was writing at about the same time as Dicey formulated his theory of the constitution and of parliamentary sovereignty. The point was well understood before this. In 1839 Lord John Russell wrote:

> Every political constitution in which different bodies share the supreme power is only enabled to exist by the forbearance of those among whom this power is distributed . . . each must exercise a wise moderation.[15]

11 Ibid, 413.
12 N. Johnson, *Reshaping the British Constitution: Essays in Political Interpretation* (2004), 2.
13 W.E. Gladstone, *Gleanings of Past Years*, vol I (1879), 245.
14 Ibid.
15 Letter of Lord John Russell to Poulett Thomson (14 October 1839), cited in Philip Shane, 'When Inter-Branch Norms Break Down: Of Arms-for-Hostages, "Orderly Shutdowns", Presidential Impeachments, and Judicial "Coups"' (2003) 12 *Cornell Journal of Law and Public Policy* 503, 508.

This third pillar of the UK's constitution continues to be important, but it does not have the same force as before.

I will discuss the interaction between these pillars in the chapters which follow. It has changed over time. Changes in the functioning and effect of each pillar put political pressure on the constitution, and that in turn potentially generates changes in constitutional doctrine and constitutional law.

Those changes in the relationship between the pillars and the associated changes in constitutional doctrine have implications for the constitutional agency of the executive, Parliament and the courts in both the senses I am using that term. They affect what each of them is authorised to do by the constitution. They also give rise to questions about which element of the constitution (Parliament, executive or courts) has the responsibility and capacity to respond in terms of doctrine and practice to a changing world in order to allow the constitution to maintain its acceptability in the eyes of the public and hence its stability.

The executive has great power under the constitution, but it is accountable to Parliament and through Parliament to the public. This control is the foundation for responsive and responsible government. Ultimate political control is through accountability to the electorate at elections. That form of control also extends in certain ways to the period before election time. Anxiety about what the electorate is thinking about policies enacted in the life of a Parliament affects political calculation and behaviour.[16]

However, by virtue of the first past the post electoral system—which tends to lead to clear and decisive parliamentary majorities—and the discipline of the party system, the executive's control over Parliament has grown. At the same time, old patterns of self-restraint and customary norms of political morality have become eroded. Attempts have been made to respond to this within Parliament through the enhancement of

16 See D. Beetham, 'Liberal Democracy and the Limits of Democratization', in D. Held (ed), *Prospects for Democracy*, (1992) *Political Studies*, Special Issue, XL, 40, at 47: 'The fact of the vote casts a long shadow in front of it', and operates as a continuous discipline on the elected.

the select committee system. But the changes also pose challenges for the courts. If control of executive power through the political system is weakened, does that call for a turn to more legal controls to be enforced by the courts? And if so, is it Parliament or the courts, or both, which have the responsibility to fashion a response?

Alongside these changes, the increase in the twentieth century of what was expected of the state in terms of the protections it would provide for its citizens in relation to health, security and welfare, and the democratic incentive for governments to respond to this, created a greatly expanded administrative state. In consequence, as well as acquiring enhanced power in relation to Parliament, the executive has acquired greater power over the lives of citizens, at the interface between state and society. That too has called for a response in terms of public law doctrine to ensure that the exercise of that power is subject to adequate and appropriate control.

The Human Rights Act 1998 has been part of Parliament's response. The development of the common law of judicial review and the principle of legality as an approach to statutory interpretation has been a response by the courts. Both have posed their own challenges in terms of integration with the democratic principle and the constitutional principle of the sovereignty of Parliament.

There are no fixed natural principles governing the organisation of a liberal democratic polity. The emergence of such a polity is a matter of contingency and relatively stable political compromise. Raymond Geuss, for example, argues[17] that the component elements of liberal democracy harbour important internal contradictions (for instance, between different conceptions of democracy) and also are in tension with each other. The rule of law, for instance, is ultimately difficult to reconcile in full with the discretion inhering in the executive and its ability to react speedily to events, which is an inevitable part of governing.[18] In a similar way, John Dunn emphasises the tension between democracy and the rule of law.[19] These are not principles which find a natural point of reconciliation; they

17 R. Geuss, *History and Illusion in Politics* (2001).
18 Ibid, 108.
19 J. Dunn, *Breaking Democracy's Spell* (2014).

support different claims and different values, and the balance between them is arrived at by compromise within particular political systems. John Gray seeks to dethrone an Enlightenment view of liberalism as a natural order based on rationality and argues instead for a view of liberalism as a *modus vivendi*, a form of life which in practice succeeds in accommodating competing values in ways which are acceptable and stable in local terms.[20] Making the same point from a legal perspective, Martin Loughlin explains how public law seeks to reconcile 'the desire to be autonomous and the desire to be a participant in a common venture'. He writes, 'this disjuncture between freedom and belonging can be neither eliminated nor reconciled, it can only be negotiated', meaning that public law 'is best expressed as an exercise in political jurisprudence . . . the discourse of political right involves the elaboration of a prudential language through which that negotiation is effected'.[21] That is a theoretical perspective well suited to the analysis of the UK constitution. It also accounts for its longevity and relative success. As David Feldman explains, 'values conflict, and the more fundamental they are, the more fundamentally they will conflict. Constitutions are, in part, processes for mediating those conflicts while allowing the state to function day to day'.[22]

Maitland observed that 'the constitution is largely defined by those institutions and practices which emerged from and were confirmed as acceptable conclusions facilitating renewal of constructive political activity after phases of acute conflict and division'.[23]

There is no foundational written constitution in the UK, so the legal rules which can be counted as constitutional tend to be more in the nature of general principles which, at certain points, achieve sufficient solidity to be enforced as legal norms. There is no specific body of law which is clearly demarcated as constitutional. Viewed as an aspect of the

20 J. Gray, *Two Faces of Liberalism* (2000). Gray writes that relinquishing the Enlightenment view 'is no loss, since it means that the diversity of ways of life and regimes is a mark of human freedom' (p 139).

21 M. Loughlin, *Foundations of Public Law* (2010), 11.

22 D. Feldman, *Key Ideas in Constitutional Law* (2025), 17.

23 Quoted in Johnson, *Reshaping*, 14–15.

public law of the state, constitutional law in the UK tends to emerge from aspects of administrative law, which is the law which has the main role in determining the powers and responsibilities of public authorities and the conditions which they have to fulfil in terms of respecting citizens' rights when making decisions. But at the same time there are statutory texts with constitutional significance. These are studded throughout the regime of administrative and constitutional law and produce concrete legal effects. British constitutional values have in turn been informed by important texts and the assimilation of statutory reforms within a common law system. These include the Magna Carta (1215), the legislation to exclude papal jurisdiction in the sixteenth century, the Petition of Right 1628, the Act to abolish the Star Chamber, the Habeas Corpus legislation, the Bill of Rights 1689, the Act of Union of 1707 and the Great Reform Act 1832 and the expansion of the franchise thereafter.[24]

Elements of constitutional law can be identified in the common law, in statute, in the way statute is embedded in and interacts with the common law, and in the prerogative and other forms of executive power. The significance of the written/unwritten distinction should not be exaggerated. There is a range of written instruments which have constitutional significance, and codified systems also depend on custom and convention.[25] For this reason Nevil Johnson emphasises other features of the British constitution which tend to make it distinctive: it is customary, conventional, traditional and informal.[26]

In general terms I would argue that the most satisfactory account of how the principles of collective self-determination and individual autonomy fit together in a way which respects the value inherent in each of them is to regard protection of individual rights as the foundation for

24 Johnson, *Reshaping*, 14–15.

25 See e.g. K. Whittington, *Constitutional Construction:* Divided *Powers and Constitutional Meaning* (1999); M. Foley, *The Silence of Constitutions: Gaps, 'Abeyances' and Political Temperament in the Maintenance of Government* (1989); A. Kavanagh, 'The Ubiquity of Unwritten Constitutionalism' (2023) 21 *International Journal of Constitutional Law* 968.

26 Johnson, *Reshaping*, 13.

genuine formation of a collective will which is worthy of respect. In this way, political authority can be said to flow upwards, from the people. John Dewey wrote:

> Majority rule, just as majority rule, is as foolish as its critics charge it with being. But it is never *merely* majority rule. As a practical politician, Samuel J. Tilden, said a long time ago: 'The means by which a majority comes to be a majority is the most important thing': antecedent debates, modification of views to meet the opinions of minorities, the relative satisfaction given to the latter by the fact that it has had a chance and that next time it may be successful in becoming a majority . . . The essential need, in other words, is the improvement of the methods and conditions of debate, discussion and persuasion. That is *the* problem of the public.[27]

David Beetham explains that the relationship between the liberal and the democratic elements in liberal democracy 'is both one of mutual necessity and a source of tension or antagonism'.[28] Many aspects of the liberal heritage are fundamental to the continuance of democracy itself, such as freedom of expression, the separation of powers and the rule of law. Also, 'To be able to shape the course or conditions of one's life through sharing control over collective decisions is a necessary counterpart to exercising such control at the personal or individual level'.[29]

There is a further aspect of the problem of the public, or the defence of the constitution, which should be emphasised. That is how the constitution can be framed in terms which inspire loyalty and emotional attachment on the part of the public. In an interesting article, Illan Wall and Daniel Matthews argue that there is an important aesthetic dimension to the construction of the sovereignty of a legal order, alongside political and legal elements.[30] I would call it the emotional dimension of loyalty to the constitution. Any constitutional order requires an element of emotional resonance to sustain public support for it. Judge Learned Hand made this point with force in relation to the US Constitution:

27 J. Dewey, *The Public and its Problems* (1927), 207–208 (emphasis in original).

28 Beetham, 'Liberal Democracy and the Limits of Democratization', 41.

29 Ibid, 45.

30 I. Wall and D. Matthews, 'Sovereignty and the Persistence of the Aesthetic' (2024) 87 *Modern Law Review* 1393.

> Liberty lies in the hearts of men and women; when it dies there, no constitution, no law, no court can save it.[31]

The need to find a focus for emotional support for the constitutional order is particularly important in the case of the UK, which does not have a constitutional instrument like the US Constitution to serve as a banner for loyalty and public attachment. Instead, the UK's constitution has to inspire loyalty through a sense that it meets public needs in terms of protection of individual interests, including by allowing fair opportunity for participation in the exercise of political control through the electoral system and to vindicate individual rights by going to court. There is also a need to seek emotional resonance in identifying its underlying value in an ethic of liberty, both at the individual and at the collective level. An historical sense that the UK's constitutional order has successfully given effect to that ethic over a long time and enabled the country to survive and thrive in a world of challenges may also be significant. I will return to this in the concluding chapter.

In a discussion of the political thought of Hannah Arendt, Christian Volk argues for a conception of the constitution which involves both law and politics, without assigning primacy to either of them.[32] According to Arendt a third element is also required. On this account the triad of constitutionalism is law, politics and a reliable political order.[33] A reliable political order cannot be realised permanently through law made by an administrative and judicial elite, separated from the processes of formation of public opinion and political action, because citizens will feel alienated from this and will be deprived of political experience, making them vulnerable to populism and authoritarian politics. On the other hand, a Rousseauean view of the primacy of politics undermines individual rights and jeopardises the reliability, predictability and stability of the political order. Law and politics are interrelated, and each must take

31 Learned Hand, speech on 21 May 1944, in *The Spirit of Liberty: Papers and Addresses of Learned Hand* (ed. Irving Dilliard, 1954), 190.

32 C. Volk, *Arendtian Constitutionalism: Law, Politics and the Order of Freedom* (2015), esp ch 5.

33 Ibid, 174.

the requirements of the other sphere into consideration.[34] The structure of order enables joint effort in political action, not through fixed pre-political rights, but as norms which originate in and are experienced as intrinsic to political action.[35] One needs both law and politics to realise the multiple goods which a constitution seeks to promote and because, as Volk puts it: 'to uphold a democratic polity is only possible through experiencing political acting'.[36] In Arendt's view political power is only formed at the moment of action between people, and it disintegrates if they do not act together.[37]

This book will argue that a constitution is not just concerned with ensuring that individual rights are protected. Its primary function is to generate authority which can be regarded as legitimate. Each of the executive, Parliament and the courts provides mutual reinforcement for each other as well as fulfilling its own particular function. An efficient executive provides effective government and ensures the implementation of the policy commitments decided upon by Parliament and the rulings of the courts. The decisions made by Parliament and the courts legitimise the direct exercise of power by the executive. Legislation by Parliament provides a framework of law for the courts to apply, thereby giving effect to choices made by democratic means. And the courts safeguard the conditions under which public opinion comes to be formed and democratic procedures reflect genuine and free consent of citizens by securing their legal rights and thus upholding freedom under the law.

34 Ibid, 175–176.
35 Ibid, 228–229.
36 Ibid, 229.
37 Ibid, 229.

2

The Constitutional Agency Exercised by the Executive

An active and effective executive arm is an essential part of the constitutional picture sketched out in chapter 1. Authority will count for nothing and the political order will lose its legitimacy if decisions taken within it, which are lawful, are not implemented.

Francis Fukuyama outlines the threat of political decay in the United States, as it becomes what he calls a 'vetocracy', in which checks and balances in the system create too many veto points and the capacity of the state for effective action is undermined.[1] The increased emphasis on what is sometimes called the 'imperial presidency' and on executive power in the American context can be seen as an attempt to break out of this impasse.[2] Fukuyama argues that constitutional design should be at least as much concerned with 'the creation of authority and the accumulation of power' as with 'the limitation of authority and the division of power'.[3] He quotes Alexander Hamilton:

> Energy in the Executive is a leading character in the definition of good government. It is essential to the protection of the community against foreign attacks; it is not less essential to the steady administration of the laws . . . A feeble execution is but another phrase for a bad execution; and a

1 F. Fukuyama, *Political Order and Political Decay: From the Industrial Revolution to the Globalisation of Democracy* (2014), ch 34.
2 See, e.g., E. Posner and A. Vermeule, *The Executive Unbound: After the Madisonian Republic* (2010).
3 Fukuyama, *Political Order and Political Decay*, epigraph, quoting Samuel P. Huntington.

Constitutional Agency. Philip Sales, Oxford University Press. © Philip Sales 2026.
DOI: 10.1093/oso/9780197928370.003.0002

> government ill executed, whatever it may be in theory, must be, in practice, a bad government.[4]

Jack Balkin makes a similar point: government must be sufficiently effective to maintain security and social peace and sufficiently just to be deserving of co-operative engagement by citizens.[5]

The effectiveness of government is linked to the capacity of the executive to respond speedily to unfolding events. As Raymond Geuss puts it, 'politics is in part about dealing with the unexpected, and one of the points of having public officials and a government at all is to allow them to respond quickly and flexibly to urgent matters that have not been anticipated.'[6]

The ability of a regime to provide a safe and reliable political and social order and to give practical effect to legal and political decisions taken according to proper procedures is an important foundation for the legitimacy of the governance system in that regime.[7] As Tony Judt writes in *Postwar*, his history of Europe after the Second World: 'Keeping citizens safe is what states do. . . . Legitimacy is a function of capacity'.[8] Writing in the same vein, John Dunn says,

> There is a need on the part of its subjects to which sovereignty answers: above all, the need to establish and sustain a framework within which they can hope to live securely.[9]

The ability to provide security and effective government is sometimes referred to as output legitimacy.[10] Therefore, legal rules preserving freedom of action for the executive can be as important as legal rules which impose positive duties on them.

With this critical point in mind, I turn to address the role of the executive in the governance system of the UK.

4 Ibid, epigraph.
5 J. Balkin, *Constitutional Redemption: Political Faith in an Unjust World* (2011), ch 3.
6 R. Geuss, *History and Illusion in Politics* (2001), 108.
7 For further discussion see P. Sales, 'Legalism in Constitutional Law: Judging in a Democracy' [2018] *Public Law* 687.
8 Tony Judt, *Postwar: A History of Europe Since 1945* (2005), 797.
9 J. Dunn, *Breaking Democracy's Spell* (2014), 19–20.
10 F. Scharpf, *Governing in Europe: Effective and Democratic?* (1999), 2–5.

The executive is the body charged with carrying on the government of the state in a fast-paced and changing world. It is constituted as a set of complex departments and bodies. It has the task of ruling, subject to the allocation of legislative functions to Parliament and judicial functions to the courts.

The executive attracts the attention of practising and academic lawyers less than Parliament and the courts, which are focused on the making and interpretation of the law.[11] The focus of the executive is on ruling, in a wider sense. But to understand how the constitution works, it is important to give it equal importance.

The executive is central to the operation of the constitutional order, through its control of parliamentary business and the legislative process, its authority to make the fundamental choices for the state regarding raising taxes and deploying state resources and its power of day-to-day rule.[12] The executive is responsive to democratic inputs through the need to win national elections and to command a majority in the House of Commons. It commands the civil service, which is the repository for expertise within the governance system and has responsibility for the implementation of policy. The executive government is responsible for the conduct of international relations and for managing the interface between international law and domestic law. It also has an extensive law-making function through the promulgation of subordinate legislation. Therefore, the executive's active agency is at the heart of making the governance system work as a vibrant and responsive liberal democratic order.

The executive government is intimately bound up with control *by* Parliament, but also control *of* Parliament. Ministers have to be Members of Parliament and are accountable to Parliament. The Prime Minister

11 See my reflections on T. Daintith and A. Page, *The Executive in the Constitution* (1999) in ch 9 of P. O'Brien and B. Yong (eds), *Leading Works in Public Law* (2025). This book by Daintith and Page is an outstanding exception.

12 The term 'executive' has a flexible meaning according to context, ranging from ministers at the apex of government, through the civil service which serves them, to other bodies which act on behalf of the state in various ways to implement policy or apply the law and which are distinct from the legislature and the courts. My focus is on ministers and the central civil service.

has to be able to command the confidence of a majority of MPs in the House of Commons, and he or she (and their government) is liable to be removed after a vote of no confidence. This is important as a potential safety valve to remove the government if it becomes seriously unpopular. But party discipline means that it is unlikely to be used where the governing party has a significant majority of MPs. Accountability to and removal by Parliament is the constitution's primary mechanism to promote responsible government. The government must respond to MPs' concerns, and MPs will be responsive to the concerns of their constituents.

At the same time, command of a majority in the House of Commons gives the executive a large measure of control over the activity of Parliament. It enables the executive to use Parliament as a tool of government.[13] It gives the executive the means to create law in its highest form, that is primary legislation. In the light of the basic legitimation demand in the modern state, law is a primary resource for effective government and the ability to create new law is fundamental.[14] Moreover, it has been observed that the executive's 'right of initiative in relation to both taxes and spending makes it the partner, not the subordinate, of Parliament'.[15]

The executive is plural in nature and has a wide variety of functions, reflecting the multifarious demands upon the state. It is not as such a legal person or a subject granted legal powers. In the *Town Investments* case Lord Simon of Glaisdale said that the term 'the executive' is 'barely known to the law'.[16] Maitland wrote that the executive is not 'a legal organisation. Of course I do not mean it is an illegal organisation; rather I should prefer to say it is an extra-legal organisation: the law does not condemn it, but it does not recognise it—knows nothing about it'.[17]

13 'The efficient secret of the English Constitution may be described as the close union, the nearly complete fusion, of the executive and legislative powers': W. Bagehot, *The English Constitution* (with an Introduction by RHS Crossman) (1963), 65.

14 Daintith and Page, *The Executive in the Constitution*, 23–24.

15 Ibid, 209.

16 *Town Investments Ltd v Department of Environment* [1978] AC 359, 398.

17 F.W. Maitland, *The Constitutional History of England* (1908), 387.

The complex concept of the Crown does some work to give a degree of legal form to the executive government, on the theory that the Crown is an abstraction of the monarch who acts on the advice of his or her ministers. But in reality the executive is a political concept. Most of its legal powers are conferred by statute on a Secretary of State, each of whom heads a distinct department. Coordination is achieved and coherence given to executive action through political control via the Cabinet, as a committee of ministers chaired by the Prime Minister.

Accordingly, an important dimension of the constitutional significance of what the executive does is this coordination effort through its own internal measures to stabilise and control the powers and discretions granted to it by the law. This is a subject explored by Daintith and Page in detail in *The Executive in the Constitution*. They explain that 'the United Kingdom executive is more plural than unitary';[18] 'the functions of modern government have been laid not on the executive as a whole but on "a heterogeneous collection of ministers, officers, and authorities exercising a mass of apparently unrelated miscellaneous functions"'.[19]

Daintith and Page explain how coherent coordination is achieved in relation to such fundamental matters as how government secures money supply from Parliament, how the executive is central to the distribution of funds voted for its use and how in practical terms it seeks to ensure, through Treasury control, that spending by government departments is directed to proper ends and is accounted for. The government has extensive control over the parliamentary procedure in relation to Money Bills and the Treasury has considerable powers of control in relation to the use of funds by Departments. The flexibility of these procedures means that the executive is able to adjust them very easily to take account of changing demands upon the system.

The internal control of the executive over itself is distinct from external control through political mechanisms (the discipline of elections and parliamentary controls) and legal mechanisms (control by the courts

18 Daintith and Page, *The Executive in the Constitution*, 6.
19 Ibid, 26, quoting Sir Ivor Jennings, *Cabinet Government* (3rd ed., 1959), 90.

through judicial review). It is very important, since Parliament and the courts do not have the capacity for continuous supervision of government. 'In consequence the effectiveness with which the values of democratic accountability and of legality are implemented in the British system depends in large measure upon the executive's being so organised and controlled as to achieve those ends.'[20] In exercising control over itself, the executive is a source of normative direction and the guardian of values which serve the ends of democratic control and the rule of law. This is done by a combination of rules laid down by the centre and by inculcating an official culture which, whilst particular to each department, looks to the centre for guidance. Through internal control the executive transforms its powers and discretions into stable rules and procedures for deploying the resources of government. Those rules and procedures are themselves an important part of constitutional practice and, in certain respects, constitutional law.

One constitutional boundary that has not emerged is between the political executive and the professional or expert executive. In the UK's constitution the executive has a dual role. On the one hand, it emerges from Parliament as the government selected by the majority party, elected on the basis of a manifesto presented to the public. This governing group has responsibility for dealing with the public finances, for the management of public affairs and for initiating legislation. It is the active element of the democratic principle, selected and maintained in power through the political process.

On the other hand, the executive is also the body which has access to the expertise of a professional cadre of civil servants maintained by the state and necessary for the effective fulfilment of a wide range of state functions. According to constitutional theory, this civil service exists as a neutral body which is in place to carry out the directions of the political executive.[21] It has not achieved an independent status of its own which

20 Ibid, 4.
21 Johnson, *Reshaping*, 94–97, 228–235.

gives it a substantial power of resistance against the political executive.[22] Instead, the executive is treated by the courts as one undifferentiated whole, represented in a typical case by a Secretary of State at the head of a government department, which has an authority to act based on a combination of the democratic principle and a principle of professional expertise.[23]

This dual character of the executive, as authorised through the democratic process to exercise political power and as expert, is increasingly reflected in the contours of the law as articulated by the courts in terms of the separation of powers: see chapter 4, on the constitutional agency exercised by the courts.

The strict legal control of tax and spending by Parliament, pursuant to the initiative of the Government acting by the Treasury, and these various mechanisms of supervision by executive and Parliament, are the foundation for democratic control of taxation and spending.[24] Treasury control of spending is one of the primary means by which the executive both pursues its own functional objectives and upholds democratic values, by ensuring that funds provided by Parliament are properly spent on the purposes intended by Parliament. Control of tax and spending is also the practical material foundation for the legal doctrine of parliamentary sovereignty.[25] It is difficult to see how that doctrine could prevail

22 The central civil service was placed on a statutory footing by the Constitutional Reform and Governance Act 2010, which requires the Minister for the Civil Service to publish a code of conduct for the civil service and prescribes that it must require civil servants 'to carry out their duties for the assistance of the administration as it is duly constituted for the time being, whatever its political complexion' and to carry out their duties with integrity, honesty, objectivity and impartiality. If a minister decides not to accept advice from the civil service about how to proceed, the relevant senior civil servant can insist that a ministerial direction is given requiring the civil service to act in compliance with it, which is a way of seeking to increase the political cost to the minister of going against the advice.

23 This dual basis for the courts to accord respect to executive judgments in various contexts has been emphasised in many cases. See, in particular, *R (Begum) v Special Immigration Appeals Commission* [2021] UKSC 7; [2021] AC 765, paras 69–70; *In re an application by the Secretary of State for Northern Ireland for Judicial Review* [2025] UKSC 47, paras 38–39.

24 Daintith and Page, *The Executive in the Constitution*, 104–105.

25 See p. 41 below.

in the long run if Parliament did not have control of these fundamental aspects of state activity and power.

Six points may be made by way of an overview.

First, the executive, in the form of the Government of the day, is central to the operation of Parliament and the democratic system more generally. In order to become the Government, a party has to garner support at elections by presenting the electorate with a programme of government and legislation. Then it has to be able to secure and maintain the confidence of a majority of MPs in Parliament.

Secondly, and in consequence of its command of a majority in Parliament, in ordinary circumstances the Government controls business in Parliament. Legislative time in Parliament is a limited resource. The executive has to have in place procedures to determine how this resource is used. Parliament is in fact a vehicle for government just as much as it is a legislature. The Government uses it as a theatre for promoting, providing a public focus for and debating its wider governmental initiatives. Government is also substantially in control of the legislative programme to be presented in Parliament. This programme is presented in the King's Speech at the start of each session of Parliament. The Government has its own department of specialist drafters of legislation, the Office of Parliamentary Counsel. They take instructions from government departments and produce detailed legislative texts to implement policy initiatives in the form of law to be enacted by Parliament.

Thirdly, the Government is, through its control of Parliament, responsible for the public finances. Its role in Parliament is central to this. Taxes can only be raised pursuant to legislative provisions. Sums can only be paid out of central funds with the authority of primary legislation. Government, through its control of the legislative process, is also responsible for adjusting legal duties imposed on public authorities (compliance with which implies financial expense) with the funding available from taxation.

The implications of this are profound. It means that it is the executive which is responsible for managing a sort of legal black hole or conceptual chasm at the heart of the constitution. Legislation imposes duties on public authorities with varying degrees of specificity as to the entitlements created under it. But the imposition of a duty does not in itself carry the financial resources needed to meet it. There is a spectrum of duties. At one end there are precise, quantified entitlements in specified circumstances, with no flexibility on the part of the relevant public authority regarding matching its financial resources with the payments to be made. In the middle there are duties which are more open-textured in form and which allow a degree of flexibility for the relevant public authority to take into account the resources available to it when deciding how to fulfil its obligations.[26] At the other end there are so-called 'target duties', which involve no specific legal liability for the public authority if it fails to find the resources to provide the services specified.[27] The marrying up of legal duties and the financial resources required to comply with them—a matter at the heart of the due operation of the constitution—is thus in essence a matter for which the executive is responsible. It has the means to seek legislation to adjust the duty side of the equation, whether by imposing or reducing duties, and it is responsible for obtaining through taxation legislation and through the appropriation and funds allocation process the financial resources needed to satisfy the duties. It is through the exercise of executive powers and discretions that the legal gap between duty and funding is bridged.

Fourthly, in a state which respects the rule of law, the executive is subject to the interpretation of the law given by the courts. But that subordination of the executive to the courts is moderated through the executive's control of Parliament. In theory, if the executive cannot live with a ruling of the courts, it can seek to modify the law by introducing and passing legislation in Parliament. But as Daintith and Page point out, this course comes with a price for the Government, in terms of use of scarce legislative time and political cost. This means that in practice the

26 See e.g. *R v Gloucestershire County Council, ex p. Barry* [1997] AC 584; cf *R v East Sussex County Council, ex p. Tandy* [1998] AC 714.

27 *R v Inner London Education Authority, ex p. Ali* (1990) 2 Admin LR 822; *R (G) v London Borough of Barnet* [2004] 2 AC 208.

executive has to recognise that the courts are a serious partner in the operation of the administration and accordingly has to take account of the distinct rule of law values which they promote.

Fifthly, the executive implements and enforces the law as laid down by Parliament and the courts. It is itself subject to and required properly to adhere to the legal rules laid down by them. Hence the executive's internal processes for taking legal advice and disseminating it are far more important than the sporadic incidence of judicial review by the courts for practical adherence to the rule of law on the ground in the myriad situations and thousands of cases the executive has to deal with day in, day out.

Sixthly, by implementing the law and providing public services in an effective way, the executive provides output legitimacy and hence reinforces the overall legitimacy of the constitution in a vital way. Also, the civil service supplies an element of legitimacy through expertise in the management of state affairs. It also provides stability in the formation and delivery of policy over time, counterbalancing to some degree the vicissitudes of democratic politics. However, for reasons to do with the culture of the British civil service, as analysed by Daintith and Page, it might still be said that the executive is better at policy formulation at the centre rather than service delivery through its various agencies and other bodies dispersed through the governmental system.

This leaves three other areas of executive action which are of particular constitutional significance: (i) the conduct of international relations and management of the interface between international law and domestic law; (ii) the executive as legislator through the promulgation of subordinate legislation; and (iii) the executive as rule-maker through the promulgation of policy guidance.

(i) International Relations

As regards the conduct of international relations, as the first *Miller* case[28] highlighted, the executive retains an important function in managing

28 *R (Miller) v Secretary of State for Exiting the European Union* [2017] UKSC 5; [2018] AC 61.

the UK's foreign relations and entering into treaties. In an increasingly interconnected world, where coordinated actions across governments are called for to address problems with international dimensions such as climate change and international security, these are important powers. For example, the executive controls the exercise of prerogative powers to declare and wage war and decides on actions to be taken in relation to international institutions.[29] Moreover, the executive is central to managing the interface between the UK's international obligations and its internal domestic legal order. If the executive negotiates treaty obligations, it has to ensure that any legislation that is necessary to ensure the UK complies with those obligations is brought before Parliament and passed into law. If the UK has entered into a treaty and ratified it, the political pressure on Parliament to pass the necessary legislation may be high. So the power of initiative for the executive government in international relations is important.

Tom Poole argues that modern states enjoy a sort of compound sovereignty, in which they are nested within and increasingly both enabled by and constrained by international law.[30] As he puts it: 'while the capacity of the state to interact "normally" with other states is enhanced as a result of this development, its effective choice-set when it comes to "sovereign" acts is more limited than it once was, when the juridical atmosphere that animated the state was thinner'.[31] Therefore, international and domestic law should be seen not as wholly distinct, but as overlapping and mutually reinforcing bodies of legal authority. It is the executive which actively manages this compound sovereignty, steering the state in its relations with others.

(ii) Subordinate Legislation

The creation of subordinate or delegated legislation is another area of profound and growing importance in terms of the power wielded by the executive within the constitution. There are substantial criticisms of the

29 Such as how to vote on the UK Security Council.
30 T. Poole, "The Constitution and Foreign Affairs" (2016) 69 *Current Legal Problems* 143.
31 Ibid, 154.

way in which law-making by subordinate legislation undermines parliamentary control, given that the standard of scrutiny is low. Already in 1929 Lord Hewart attacked the delegation of legislative power,[32] but that attack did not lead to the curtailment of that power. No government has reversed this trend. Indeed, the transfer of legislative power to the executive has increased.

The standard justifications for delegated legislation are that: (i) use of delegated legislation is necessary because of the limits on parliamentary time for creating primary legislation; (ii) use of delegated legislation may be necessary where it is desirable for laws to be drafted by reference to specialist expertise which may more readily be available within a Government department; and (iii) delegated legislation may more readily meet the need for flexibility and expedition on occasion in the interests of effective government.

It also seems broadly desirable that big-picture policy issues for legislation should usually be set out in primary legislation, debated in Parliament and subject to amendment procedures in the usual way, whereas it is more appropriate for fine detail to be pushed down into delegated legislation.

Further, it seems sensible to allow for different levels of oversight by Parliament of delegated legislation. This allows for more finely calibrated accommodations between democratic oversight by Parliament and the values promoted by the use of delegated legislation and parliamentary time-saving made possible by such use. This is what the various gradations of parliamentary oversight are designed to achieve, moving from the simple laying of some forms of delegated rules before Parliament (so that Parliament is afforded an opportunity to intervene, if it chooses), through the negative resolution procedure and the affirmative resolution procedure, and on to the super-affirmative resolution procedure for certain kinds of delegated legislation. It should be noted that there has been a movement towards graduated parliamentary involvement at the level of primary legislation level as well, with special truncated parliamentary

32 G. Hewart, *The New Despotism* (1929).

procedures for certain kinds of uncontroversial legislation or legislation proposed by the Law Commission.

This makes it sound as though there is a coherent scheme which governs law-making and the relationship between primary and secondary legislation. The problem is that this scheme does not survive contact with the real world of politics. It appears that in reality there is very little effective parliamentary scrutiny.[33]

The principal reasons for this, I suggest, are threefold. First, there is the increase in governmental activity since the nineteenth century. Rule by central government has massively expanded due to the demands made on the state for welfare protection, provision of health services, management of the economy, management of various security risks and so forth as a result of the democratisation of our political system. To this must be added the boost to centralisation through the experience of two World Wars. It is noticeable how even in the course of the nineteenth century the form of legislation changed, with fewer and fewer Acts of Parliament to regulate purely local matters than had previously been the case.[34] How much more so is that true in the twentieth and twenty-first centuries.

The second reason, which is connected with the first, is the limits on parliamentary time and the demands made on that limited time. The increase in the grant of powers to create subordinate legislation is a response to the fact that legislative time in Parliament is a highly constrained resource. The grant of these powers can be seen as a sort of safety valve to ensure the executive can produce binding law to carry on governance

33 See J. King, 'The Province of Delegated Legislation', ch 8 in E. Fisher et al (eds), *The Foundations and Future of Public Law: Essays in Honour of Paul Craig* (2020); M. Russell, 'Should We Be Worried About the Decline of Parliamentary Scrutiny?' [2025] *Public Law* 31; and, e.g., the 12th Report of Session 2021–2022 of the House of Lords' Delegated Powers and Regulatory Reform Committee, *Democracy Denied? The Urgent Need to Eebalance Power between Parliament and the Executive.*

34 Cf F.W. Maitland, *The Constitutional History of England* ([1909] 1941), 383; P. Sales and B. Hooper, 'Proportionality and the Form of Law' (2003) 119 *Law Quarterly Review* 426, 453–454.

despite the existence of legislative hold-ups in taking primary legislation through an overburdened Parliament.

As already mentioned, Parliament is an instrument of government as well as a legislature. It is the site for political debate and theatre, providing a focus for democratic engagement and scrutiny. It is the place for important government announcements, for debate over government policy, for holding the government to account and—ultimately—for testing the ability of governments to rule, by holding votes of confidence. It is the hurly burly of the political contest which, unsurprisingly, tends to capture the time and attention of politicians and the wider public, rather than the legal minutiae of legislation. MPs' attention is most concentrated on legislation at those points where the legislation itself becomes the focus for more general public discussion and attention. None of this is wrong or necessarily bad. The profile and focus which the more theatrical elements of politics give to public debate regarding the general policy direction of government are an important concomitant of an effectively functioning representative democracy. They provide a salient demonstration of what is being done in society's name and help connect public opinion to the political and law-making process. They assist the formation of public opinion into coherent patterns, stable across time, which in turn provide guidance for politicians in offering policy solutions, standards against which their performance in serving the public can be judged and a degree of transparency for the public to monitor the performance of their representatives.

The third reason is the basic point made by Daintith and Page about the importance of law as a resource of government in a state which is subject to the rule of law. Government needs law in order to govern legitimately and hence effectively.

So, although the abstract scheme for graduated parliamentary scrutiny and control of delegated legislation seems coherent enough, it does not work well in practice. The different grades of parliamentary oversight do not seem to act as triggers for increasing levels of scrutiny. The impression given by the statistics is that there is close to being one level of scrutiny, which is none.

Brexit highlighted and compounded the problem.[35] The parliamentary political theatre around this issue sucked up large amounts of parliamentary time and it is conceivable it may do so again from time to time. It absorbed huge amounts of politicians' time and attention outside parliamentary procedures, as they tried to explain their competing visions and compete for public support. This was entirely understandable, given the strategic importance of working out a new path forward for the country. Further, coming after years of cutting back government departments through sustained austerity policies, Brexit also put (and continues to put) special strain on the limited resources of government to work out the details of policy and give proper instructions for the drafting of primary legislation. The Office of Parliamentary Counsel, responsible for the drafting of primary legislation, has likewise been subject to cuts.

Parliament itself plainly could not cope, in addition, with the huge amount of detailed and often technical legislation which is likely to be needed to achieve the unscrambling of the UK's laws from the EU's after a period of more than 40 years of their being increasingly entwined. Given the extent of the task of this unscrambling and its importance for providing legal stability and the predictability necessary for individuals and businesses to plan their affairs, the demand for legislation is great. The position is worse if proposals to make any changes to primary legislation are remotely controversial—as many measures for effective government have to be—because that would create an even greater demand for parliamentary time for the debate necessary to carry them through Parliament. The legislator, in the form of Parliament making primary legislation, is absent, because the time and other resources needed for legislating are highly constrained and its attention is elsewhere.[36]

35 So did the use of regulatory powers during the Covid-19 crisis: see the *Final Report of the Independent Commission on UK Public Health Emergency Powers*, set up by the Bingham Centre on the Rule of Law (15 May 2024), ch 5, and *A Report by the Rt Hon the Baroness Hallett DBE, Chair of the UK Covid-19 Inquiry, on Core Decision-making and Political Governance* (the Module 2, 2A, 2C report of the inquiry) (20 November 2025), ch 13.

36 See further P. Sales, 'Law, Democracy and the Absent Legislator', ch 10 in E. Fisher, J. King and A. Young (eds), *The Foundations and Future of Public Law: Essays in Honour of Paul Craig* (2020).

(iii) Policy Guidance

In addition to subordinate legislation, an increasingly important function of the executive is the promulgation of policies to explain how ministers will exercise broad discretionary powers granted to them by Parliament. The development of the doctrine of legitimate expectations means that these policies may have an effect bordering on the legislative, by imposing defeasible legal obligations on decision-makers.[37] The promulgation of policies is not subject to parliamentary control, other than in the general sense that they might be criticised in Parliament in the same way that government can be criticised there for any of its activities. So here also the executive's constitutional role appears to be expanding.

The resort to policy guidance as a means to impose quasi-legislative control over the exercise of discretionary governmental powers allows for greater flexibility, since it is easy for statements of policy to be amended, and is in part, like the use of subordinate legislation, a response to the pressure on legislative time referred to above. The increased centrality of government by policy, rather than law, is a challenge under a constitution which is founded on the principle of the rule of law. The courts have therefore reacted to this phenomenon to impose basic standards regarding the formulation of policy statements, to ensure that they do not lead officials to act unlawfully[38] and to treat them as having strong (albeit defeasible) binding force in relation to officials in the interests of promoting the exercise of administrative powers in a way in which the public can have trust.[39] In these ways, the constitutional principle of the rule of law has been adapted to accommodate this partially formalised type of governance. At the same time, the courts have adhered to the basic distinction between law and policy, holding that policy cannot be used to modify law.[40]

37 See e.g. *United Policy Holders Group v Attorney General of Trinidad and Tobago* [2016] UKPC 17; [2016] 1 WLR 3383 and further discussion in chapter 4.

38 See *R (A) v Secretary of State for the Home Department* [2021] UKSC 37.

39 See, e.g., *Mandalia v Secretary of State for the Home Department* [2015] UKSC 15; [2015] 1 WLR 4546, discussed in chapter 4.

40 *C.G. Fry & Son Ltd v Secretary of State for Housing, Communities and Local Government* [2025] UKSC 35.

Other Executive Bodies in the UK

The focus of this chapter has been on the executive which constitutes the central government of the state. There are bodies outside central government which have public powers conferred upon them and which therefore play a part in the administration of the state. Leaving aside the devolved legislatures and administrations (which are a huge and complex topic outside the scope of this book), two sets of other public authorities can be regarded as part of the executive of the state in a wider sense and should be mentioned here in order to locate them in this discussion of constitutional agency. They are (i) local government and (ii) independent regulatory authorities.

(i) Local Government

The UK has always had an elaborate system of local government, with governing authorities at various levels. Up to the latter part of the twentieth century the UK's constitutional arrangements could be regarded as having a strong local orientation. A good deal of active government occurred at the local level, where local authorities had significant tax-raising powers and significant discretion in relation to spending those taxes and how to govern within their areas. Governance at this level, and in particular the ability to tax and spend, was subject to political control through local democracy, involving the election of councilors who, according to a principle of majority rule, would then seek to form the local governing body. This meant a form of responsible government existed at local level along similar lines to that which existed at national level. There was, in the words of Nevil Johnson, 'a heritage of diffused powers' at the level of local government which had real force and depth, so that 'the British constitution . . . underpinned a structure of government that was in some degree unified rather than unitary', by contrast with the model of continental European states.[41] There was a rejection of the notion of

41 Johnson, *Reshaping*, 40–41.

a strong executive role for central government, and instead 'there was a desire to leave the provision of most services (which were in any case on a very modest scale indeed) to authorities and agencies quite separate from the central institutions'.[42]

This meant that the British state had strong characteristics of administrative and political pluralism, but the traditional blend proved to be unstable, as state services financed by central government expanded (particularly in the form of the welfare state). This created pressure for standards of provision which were equalised across the nation and meant that there was an increased focus of the political system upon acquisition of power at the centre by competing national parties seeking to meet the expectations of the electorate.[43] The localised model of the British constitution which was such a marked feature of the earlier period has therefore been superseded by the demands of national politics and a concentration of power at the centre.

This tendency to concentrate power at the centre became particularly marked in the period of Conservative government between 1979 and 1997, in which local government was restructured. Martin Loughlin observes that the effect of this 'was to bring to an end the constitutional significance of local government in the British system'.[44] Local government has many functions imposed on it by legislation and so acts as an important vehicle for delivery of national policies (e.g. in relation to provision of social housing) which are funded in large part by annual grants from central government. However, under conditions of financial stress and national political pressure to limit taxes, local government is caught in the legal black hole described above, in which it often suits central government to impose duties upon local authorities without necessarily providing the full resources needed to meet those obligations.

There are two consequences. First, through financial constraint, the scope for local democratic influence on outcomes produced by local

42 Ibid, 141.
43 Ibid, 49–51.
44 M. Loughlin, 'Evolution and Gestalt of the State in the United Kingdom', ch 13 in A. von Bogdandy et al (eds), *The Administrative State*, vol I (2017), 489.

authorities has become attenuated. Local authorities often do not have much genuine discretion to exercise in deciding how to govern in their areas. Instead, they are left desperately trying to match the resources given to them by central government with the obligations imposed on them by central government. Second, the courts have increasingly had to find ways to formulate doctrine to manage the pressures bearing on local authorities, which balance the demands of the rule of law with a recognition of practical constraints.[45]

The effect of this development is that local authorities no longer have constitutional agency to any significant degree in either of the senses indicated in chapter 1.

(ii) Independent Regulatory Agencies

In certain contexts the state has found it necessary to create regulatory bodies which are deliberately insulated from the political pressures to which the central executive government is subject. This is particularly the case where the state relies on market mechanisms to raise money for itself or where it wishes to structure markets in the interests of consumers. Such regulatory bodies are also a mechanism used to seek to ensure impartial and effective enforcement of important norms with constitutional significance, to foster trust on the part of the public that those norms are indeed being respected without the risk of them being waived in particular cases for partisan political advantage. Tarun Khaitan refers to these regulators as guarantor institutions.[46]

The grant of independence to the Bank of England in 1997 is a prime example of the use of this technique as a mechanism to reassure markets. Various regulators such as the Competition and Markets Authority and those for the water and power industries (Ofwat, Ofgem and so on) are examples of the use of regulators to structure markets and enforce market rules in the interests of consumers. Typically, this is done to foster trust

45 e.g., see *R (Imam) v London Borough of Croydon* [2023] UKSC 45; [2025] AC 335.

46 T. Khaitan, 'Guarantor Institutions' (2021) 16 *Asian Journal of Comparative Law* (Supplement S1).

over the long term and ensure neutral application of relevant consumer protection standards by experts, which reinforce the effective operation of markets. The phenomenon is analysed by Frank Vibert in *The Rise of the Unelected*.[47]

There is a growing number of guarantor institutions in the UK context, such as the Electoral Commission, the Equality and Human Rights Commission, the Boundaries Commissions (which establish parliamentary constituency boundaries), the Ethics and Integrity Commission (to oversee ethics in public life) and the Judicial Appointments Commissions. Their expansion can be seen as a response, in part, to the erosion of trust in informal political conventions and morality to which reference was made in chapter 1. Their function is to provide a credible and enduring guarantee that particular norms of constitutional significance will be respected, such as that constituency boundaries will be set by reference to neutral criteria and without gerrymandering and that judges should be appointed on the basis of their merit as lawyers rather than for political reasons.[48]

It can be said that this set of independent bodies is an important way in which the modern British state is structured and that they represent a fourth pillar of the constitution, alongside Parliament, the executive and the courts. They clearly have significant discretionary powers of judgment about how to regulate in their assigned areas, and to that extent exercise agency. But they are given specific and targeted roles, and they operate within the confines of those assigned roles. They do not exercise a wider form of constitutional agency in the sense being discussed in this book. What they do illustrate is the power of the executive, acting by

47 F. Vibert, *The Rise of the Unelected: Democracy and the New Separation of Powers* (2007). See also P. Tuck, *Unelected Power: The Search for Legitimacy in Central Banking and the Regulatory State* (2019).

48 Another of the guarantor institutions is the parliamentary ombudsman, who has power to investigate and give redress in relation to administrative failures, reinforcing political controls over the administration. But their role is made subordinate to that of the courts in conducting judicial review: see *Re McAleenon* [2024] UKSC 31; [2025] AC 1362. This reflects the basic shift to the law, and away from politics, as the primary mechanism of individual redress in relation to such failures.

itself or using the vehicle of Parliament, to take action to structure the constitutional environment in important ways.

Conclusion

The constitutional role of the executive tends to be overlooked in law books, because a lot of that role does not involve law as such. But the executive has a good claim to be the most important body which exercises constitutional agency in both the senses elaborated in chapter 1. It provides the animating spirit of the constitution.

The executive government has a wealth of legal powers for action available to it, under the prerogative, under the common law and as conferred by statute. The legal controls in relation to these will be discussed in chapter 4, on the constitutional agency exercised by the courts. These powers allow the executive to exercise constitutional agency across a wide range.

Most fundamentally, the executive is responsible for the active management of the implementation of the constitutional order. Central to this is its responsibility for managing taxation and spending through the formation of government policy, obtaining funds from Parliament, matching legal responsibilities of public bodies with the funds available to them and ensuring that the funds provided are spent in accordance with Parliament's will.

Finally, through its practical control of legislation in Parliament, the executive has the power to effect constitutional change of the most far-reaching kind. The enactment of the Human Rights Act 1998 is a prime example. So are the European Communities Act 1972 and the EU (Withdrawal) Act 2018. But this is agency exercised by the executive through and in partnership with Parliament. The constitutional agency exercised by Parliament and the courts must take account of the power of the executive and the need for that to be subject to controls, but also of its responsibilities and the need for it to be effective in what it does.

3

Parliament as Constitutional Agent

Parliament has a long history as the body which represents the nation and has full law-making power in respect of it. The doctrine of the sovereignty of Parliament also has a deep history in the UK's constitutional law.[1]

The idea of the sovereignty of Parliament is a claim for full agency for Parliament in terms of making laws. That is not the same as full constitutional agency, because Parliament does not govern. It acts to make laws in response to proposals put before it by members, typically those who form the government. The executive has wider constitutional agency, in the sense of the power to act and get things done. As I explained in chapter 2, the executive government, through its control of parliamentary procedure based upon its support by a majority of MPs,[2] has prior agency in terms of securing legislation. It has the power of initiative in presenting legislative proposals to Parliament to activate Parliament's law-making power.

The difficulty of Parliament exercising constitutional agency in this wider sense was demonstrated by the problems encountered during the Brexit period in 2019. Part of the problem was that the arguments about

1 J. Goldsworthy, *The Sovereignty of Parliament: History and Philosophy* (1999).

2 Which the executive may in practice be able to command, through the processes of party discipline.

Constitutional Agency. Philip Sales, Oxford University Press. © Philip Sales 2026.
DOI: 10.1093/oso/9780197928370.003.0003

Brexit cut across party lines, so the established parliamentary procedures, as framed over a long period to reflect and accommodate disagreement on a party versus party basis, were not designed to deal with the situation which arose. So great was the controversy within Parliament and within the ruling Conservative party regarding the form of the Brexit arrangements with the European Union that for a comparatively brief time the government of the day lost control of the parliamentary process and groups of MPs tried to come together to legislate for a different policy. The groups lacked internal coherence and failed in that endeavour.[3] This was an object lesson in how constitutional agency and legislative initiative are generally dependent on the prior activity of political parties in producing coherent policy proposals and then of the executive in carrying them through Parliament.

Nonetheless, the executive government does not have the power to enact primary legislation. It has to seek to persuade Parliament to do that. Parliament is a representative institution which is the embodiment of the democratic principle in the constitution. Democratic deliberation implies the possibility of choice and change.

Claude Lefort writes:

> the important point is that democracy is instituted and sustained by the *dissolution of the markers of certainty*. It inaugurates a history in which people experience a fundamental indeterminacy as to the basis of power, law and knowledge, and as to the basis of relations between *self* and *other*, at every level of social life . . . a process of questioning is implicit in social practice, that no one has the answer to the questions that arise, and the work of ideology, which is always dedicated to the task of restoring certainty, cannot put an end to this practice.[4]

Hans Kelsen, in his work of 1929, *The Essence and Value of Democracy*, similarly defended democratic parliamentary rule on the grounds of a principle of freedom.[5] The principle of freedom is also the basis of the

3 See further the discussion of the *Miller* cases in chapter 4.

4 C. Lefort, *Democracy and Political Theory* ([1986], trans David Macey 1988), 19.

5 H. Kelsen, *The Essence and Value of Democracy* ([1929], eds N. Urbinati and C. I. Accetti, trans B Graf, 2013), Editors' Introduction, 5.

demand for political equality which is central to democracy. If I am free, what gives someone the right to rule over me? All must have an equal share in the exercise of ultimate political power through the ballot box. Freedom to choose is important because there is no objective standard of political truth available on which all agree, so the idea of democracy presupposes a pluralistic perspective regarding values.[6] The circumstances of politics involve a need for collective action by people who share a common life but in circumstances where there may be deep disagreement about what should be done.[7] On Kelsen's account, in societies which are pluralistic, with no consensus belief in absolute truth and absolute values, only relative truths and values are available to human cognition. As he puts it, 'The metaphysical-absolutistic worldview is linked to an autocratic and the critical-relativistic to a democratic disposition'; everyone's political will is valued equally; there is equal regard for political opinions; and the right to govern depends on competition for public support.[8]

David Beetham makes the same point. On his account of liberal democracy, it is based on an epistemological premise that there is no final, incontestable truth about what is good for society. The only criterion of the public good is what the people, freely organised, may collectively choose. It is not for some expert or expert elite to stipulate what is the public good, since they have no claim to superior knowledge of this. Both the liberal element and the democratic element in liberal democracy are inherently antipaternalistic.[9] Both accounts nonetheless presuppose that moral value attaches to the continuance of the conditions under which free choices are able to be made.

In the light of intractable moral disagreements in modern pluralist societies, constitutional theory has moved away from natural law–inspired

6 Ibid, 7–8.

7 J. Waldron, *Law and Disagreement* (1999), 102.

8 Kelsen, *Essence and Value*, 103.

9 D. Beetham, 'Liberal Democracy and the Limits of Democratization', in D. Held (ed), *Prospects for Democracy*, (1992) *Political Studies*, Special Issue, XL, 40, at 41–42.

accounts which stressed the protection of a substantive list of metaphysically grounded pre-political individual rights and the natural ordering of society.[10] Neither judges nor politicians have superior moral knowledge regarding the right ordering of society.[11] Social values have to be constructed politically. 'Law is acknowledged to be a human construct, devised by humans according to their own self-defined purposes'.[12] In modern societies democratic self-government is the means for achieving that.

But Kelsen also noted that democratic self-government is only possible within the framework of a constitutional order. 'The people' does not exist as a reified sociological entity. It requires a set of legal procedures to determine how it can express itself and therefore govern. 'Kelsen's point is that democratic self-government is possible only within the framework of a constitutional order, because this is what defines the procedures that enable the people to govern themselves in the first place'; 'the democratic process is a form of constitutionalised politics, inasmuch as rules and procedures are essential for making it work'; the same procedures which make the expression of the popular will possible in the first place also function as limits on what it can legitimately be taken to be; so popular sovereignty is limited by the logic of its own exercise.[13] In previous work I put it this way: the constitutional rules are the grammar of the system, which enable a coherent and legitimate form of collective will to come into being.[14]

10 Christopher F. Zurn, *Deliberative Democracy and the Institutions of Judicial Review* (2007), 7.

11 Ibid, 52.

12 M. Loughlin, *Foundations of Public Law* (2010), 7, citing M. Gauchet, *The Disenchantment of the World: A Political History of Religion* (Oscar Burge trans, 1997), 28.

13 Kelsen, *Essence and Value*, Editors' Introduction, 17. In 'Liberal Democracy and the Limits of Democratization', at 44, Beetham points out that while scope for democratic critique of liberalism is necessary, it is also problematic if it threatens liberal democracy itself.

14 P. Sales, "Legalism in Constitutional Law: Judging in a Democracy" [2018] *Public Law* 687.

The History of Parliament's Constitutional Agency

We have arrived at these views about the importance of democracy after a long process of the development of ideas. Democracy was a derogatory word at the end of the eighteenth century. It came to be the dominant paradigm of government only towards the end of the nineteenth century and into the twentieth.[15] In the UK, this ideological process was linked with the expansion of the franchise.

But the history of Parliament's constitutional agency as the dominant law-making body is much longer than this. I would highlight five stages.

First, in medieval times, statutes were treated as having a place alongside or almost as part of the common law. They were like judgments of a high court, to be woven into the fabric of the common law as a whole. They could be used, like caselaw, as a foundation for analogical reasoning.

Second, a decisive change occurred in Tudor times. Henry VIII and Thomas Cromwell used Parliament and legislation to give legitimacy to the Henrician break from Rome. As Chris Thornhill writes, during the English Reformation, 'the principle of rule by the king-in-parliament became a key legitimating device of royal government'.[16] This meant that Parliament's own authority was enhanced, with the consequence that the courts began to treat the will of Parliament as expressed in the words it used in statutes as having special force. Alan Cromartie explains that 'One sign that people were impressed by parliamentary power was that they placed increasing stress on parliament's historical intentions.'[17]

Third, the Glorious Revolution of 1688 affirmed the dominance of Parliament over the Crown. The absolutist form of monarchy which was becoming more prevalent on the continent and which Charles II

15 J. Dunn, *Setting the People Free: The Story of Democracy* (2005).

16 C. Thornhill, *A Sociology of Constitutions* (2011), p. 97; Also see Duxbury, note 1 above, p. 24.

17 A. Cromartie, *The Constitutionalist Revolution: An Essay on the History of England, 1450–1642* (2006), 102–103.

and James II were seeking to copy was decisively curbed. The Bill of Rights of 1689 removed any suggestion that the monarch had a power of dispensation from statutory law. The settlement of 1688/89 affirmed that Parliament alone had the power to impose taxes and to vote money supply from the consolidated fund. This control of tax and spending provides the material foundation for the doctrine of parliamentary sovereignty which reached its fully developed form in the canonical statement by Dicey in the late nineteenth century.[18] Maitland ascribes particular importance to Parliament's control not just of raising taxes, but of spending, through the appropriation of supplies.[19] Control of taxation and appropriation by Parliament coincided with the decisive constitutional position arising in the seventeenth century, which Maitland said is the period which may be regarded 'as finally settling the sovereignty of England in king and parliament'.[20] Article 9 of the Bill of Rights protected parliamentary processes from challenge in the courts. The Act of Settlement of 1701 represented the use of Parliament's authority to modify the line of succession to the throne.

Fourth, the positivist approach to statutory interpretation was powerfully reinforced in the course of the nineteenth century. Three factors were particularly significant. First, growing adherence to a concept of parliamentary sovereignty and supremacy, culminating in Dicey's exposition. Secondly, the growing force of democratic ideology, linked to the expansion of the franchise. Thirdly, as Neil Duxbury explains in his *Elements of Legislation*,[21] a loss of confidence on the part of the judiciary

18 See T. Harris, *Revolution: The Great Crisis of the British Monarchy, 1685-1720* (2006), 353: after the Glorious Revolution 'the preferred means of keeping the crown dependent upon parliament seems to have been through the power of the purse . . . Ultimately, however, it was the financial revolution that came in the wake of William's wars, and the resultant national debt which had to be serviced by regular grants of parliamentary taxation, that guaranteed regular meetings of parliament after the Glorious Revolution'.

19 F.W. Maitland, *The Constitutional History of England* (1908), 309–310. See also A. Tomkins, *Our Republican Constitution* (2005), 107; Tony Prosser, 'The Economic Constitution', ch 4 in P. Cane and H. Kumarasingham (eds), *The Cambridge Constitutional History of the United Kingdom*, vol I (2023), 92–95.

20 Maitland, *Constitutional History*, 302; as opposed to its residing in the king alone or in the common law, as Sir Edward Coke sought to assert: ibid, 297–306.

21 N. Duxbury, *Elements of Legislation* (2012).

in the face of greater parliamentary access to and consideration of sources of information regarding social problems. Duxbury dates this to the early part of the nineteenth century. The judges felt less well informed than Parliament and so were reluctant to develop the law by reference to policy, so that the common law was seen as increasingly subordinate to statute.[22]

The fifth stage is the growth in the welfare state, and the financial commitments of the state in the twentieth and twenty-first centuries mean that parliamentary control of tax and spend has increased the practical power and authority of Parliament. Combined with the fact that the judges are not constitutionally in a position to second-guess the choices made by Parliament, the loss of confidence referred to by Duxbury, and the Kelsenian sense that in a world of pluralistic values what matters is authoritative democratic choice to prioritise certain values over others, this has tended to reinforce acceptance of the sovereignty of Parliament.

The Sovereignty of Parliament

The sovereignty of Parliament is the subject of Part 1 of Dicey's *Law of the Constitution*. It means that 'Parliament has the right to make or unmake any law whatever; and further, that no person or body is recognised by the law of England as having a right to override or set aside the legislation of Parliament'.[23] Strictly speaking, 'Parliament' is the King, the House of Lords and the House of Commons acting together. However, under modern practice, the King is a mere cipher and figurehead, and the elected House of Commons is the dominant element which is capable of enforcing its will on matters of policy and legislation.[24]

22 Ibid, 33–34.

23 A.V. Dicey, *Introduction to the Study of the Law of the Constitution* (8th ed), 38.

24 The Parliament Acts 1911 and 1949 removed the veto of the House of Lords, which now only has the power to delay the passage of legislation. When that power is exercised is a matter governed by political conventions.

Prior to Brexit, the European Communities Act 1972, which gave domestic legal effect to the UK's membership of the European Union, made a major inroad on the principle of parliamentary sovereignty. It gave the courts authority to disapply UK legislation which was incompatible with EU law. However, even then parliamentary sovereignty as such continued, in that this effect was the product of the interpretation of the 1972 Act and it was at all times possible for that Act to be amended or repealed.[25]

The principle of parliamentary sovereignty means that the distinction between constituent and constituted power is collapsed in the UK. The prominence of the conventional or customary aspect of the UK's constitution arises from this fact. As Nevil Johnson writes, 'it has been difficult, and perhaps logically impossible, to sustain a formal constitution in Britain, since in that case the terms of the constitution would have to take precedence over the claims of Parliament'.[26] The implication of this is that to a large degree constitutional *law* has to be approached in the guise of statutory interpretation. Constitutional norms, including those found to be implicit in legislation, can always in theory be overridden by ordinary legislation expressed in sufficiently clear terms.

The effect is that the constitution is flexible and can readily adjust in the light of changing political forces and circumstances. This makes it resilient. But it also means that it is more vulnerable to change and manipulation on the initiative of the executive, through its control over the legislative process.

25 *R v Secretary of State for Transport, ex p Factortame Ltd* [1990] 2 AC 85. From this perspective, the UK's membership of the EU was not so much a surrender of sovereignty as a choice about how to use it, in order to secure the benefits of cooperation with other states through that membership. The same is true of any treaty arrangement under which the UK accepts binding obligations under international law, which limit the ways in which it may use its sovereign power. The basic sovereignty of the British state continues in both cases, as Brexit showed: cf R. Tuck, *The Sleeping Sovereign: The Invention of Modern Democracy* (2016).

26 N. Johnson, *Reshaping the British Constitution* (2004), 103.

The Conventional Aspect of the Constitution and the Role of Political Parties and MPs

Nevil Johnson observes that the conventional aspect of the constitution has implications for the style of constitutionalism and constitutional law in the UK:

> The language of constitutionalism is something like a conversation within a tradition of argument about how society should be governed, whilst the language of constitutional law tends to be in terms of underlying principles as stated in the constitution and such deductions from them as specialists in constitutional law might make.[27]

At the political level, much of this conversation takes place within and between political parties. Kelsen emphasised the importance of political parties as central to modern forms of democracy. They bring people together to decide on coherent proposals for government in order to secure actual influence in shaping public affairs.[28]

In the UK in particular, the sense that national identity is expressed through Parliament is bound up with the role that political parties play in the political system.[29] Erskine May argued that contestation through the party system underpinned the freedoms of the polity. Robert Crowcroft explains that through the party system 'Deep antagonisms could be fought to a legitimate resolution' and that political parties carve out and safeguard a vital space for practical pluralism and a multiplicity of views, making it possible to arrive at clear choices which can be offered to the electorate and giving cohesion to the executive.[30] Where governments had the numbers in the House of Commons they could act with vigour, which incentivised ambitious politicians to appeal to a large section of the electorate, and party platforms offered an instrument through which

27 Ibid, 18–19.
28 Kelson, *Essence and Value*, 38.
29 See R. Crowcroft, 'Political Parties', ch 17 in P. Cane and H. Kumarasingham (eds), *The Cambridge Constitutional History of the United Kingdom*, vol I (2023).
30 Ibid, 452.

voters might judge success and failure; moreover, since leaders were vulnerable to pressures from followers, and their position was dependent on merit, parties acted as a crucial check on the executive.[31] Also, the presence of an opposition meant there was a credible alternative government which could quickly replace a government which was voted out of office.[32] Party competition strengthens Parliament as a national representative institution, since its responsiveness to public problems serves to reaffirm its authority and legitimacy; and since parties competed to control this institution rather than reform it, this contributed to stability and the possibility of peaceful political change.[33]

The Brexit debate cut across party lines. That is one reason why it proved to be somewhat indigestible in constitutional terms: the function of established political parties in a democracy to provide a regulated form of rivalry[34] broke down. Another is that parliamentary democracy is representative democracy, whereas the politics of Brexit involved an appeal to direct democracy in the form of a referendum. This imposed a significant political constraint on the agency of Parliament itself.

The fact that the UK is a parliamentary democracy, rather than a plebiscitary democracy, defines the relationship between MPs and their constituents. MPs are not delegates mandated by their constituents to vote in a particular way. They are representatives, who vote on behalf of their constituents but exercising their own judgment regarding the common good, even if that diverges from the views of their constituents. This was explained famously by Edmund Burke in his 'Address to the Electors of Bristol'.[35] The constitutional form of democracy in the UK is therefore representative rather than direct.

The touchstone for the selection of the Prime Minister and the executive government is whether they can command a majority in Parliament

31 Ibid, 452.
32 Ibid, 452.
33 Ibid, 453.
34 See N. Rosenblum, *On the Side of the Angels: An Appreciation of Parties and Partisanship* (2008), 119–126.
35 In E. Burke, *Burke's Politics; Selected Writings and Speeches of Edmund Burke on Reform, Revolution and War* (R. Hoffman and P. Levack, eds) (1949).

on key issues of policy, and in normal times Parliament is typically a vehicle for government by the executive. In that way executive and democratic power is usually aligned. But through the breakdown of party discipline under the pressure of Brexit that alignment fell apart.

A Constitutional Analysis of the Brexit Saga

It is possible to offer an analysis of the Brexit saga in democratic and constitutional terms.

By choosing to put the Brexit question to a national referendum, David Cameron's government created a tension between the principle of representative democracy by which the UK is governed and a principle of direct or plebiscitary democracy. Referendums are not without precedent in the UK, but British constitutional law does not give them a substantive role.

There is a clear mismatch between their formal legal status and their practical political effect. The formal legal status of the 2016 Brexit referendum was that it was advisory only. The government and MPs could choose to ignore it. But its practical political status was essentially as a trump card. The government made promises that it would abide by the result. MPs recognised that, whatever they might think about the merits of Brexit, contrary to Edmund Burke's account, their hands were largely tied in terms of endorsing something which could be *called* Brexit, and they were very vulnerable to political narratives designed to treat anything less than a hard form of Brexit as no Brexit at all.

The political slogan 'Brexit means Brexit' was not enlightening. However, the slogan had undeniable political power. For MPs to apply their own judgment against this would risk discrediting democracy as a principle. The general public had been invited to vote on the question and could not be expected to make nice distinctions regarding the precise constitutional status of what they had done. MPs therefore had to struggle to try to reconcile the constitutional principle of representative democracy with the alien principle of direct democracy.

The principle of the sovereignty of Parliament, insofar as it is connected with its nature as an institution of representative democracy, came under pressure as the government then sought to give effect to the Brexit vote in a way which would command acceptance with the public, first and foremost, but also with a majority of MPs. There was an important complicating factor. As part of a deal for coalition government in 2010, the Conservatives under David Cameron had agreed to legislation which set a fixed 5-year term for an elected Parliament, subject only to a vote of MPs before that end date to call for a general election or to register no confidence in the government.[36]

Under the old rules, if a government could not get a major policy through Parliament, the Prime Minister was entitled to seek the dissolution of Parliament to put the issue to the test in a general election, with the aim of securing sufficient backing in the country to get a majority of MPs to support the policy through Parliament. Theresa May, who succeeded Mr Cameron as Prime Minister, secured the authorisation from Parliament as stipulated in the new law in order to hold a general election in 2017, in which she hoped to secure a commanding majority for her particular proposed version of Brexit. But her gamble misfired, and the Parliament which was returned was one in which there was no clear majority for any version of Brexit, but also one in which MPs felt that—unusually—they, rather than the government, were in the driving seat so far as making policy on this issue was concerned.

Boris Johnson, the Prime Minister who succeeded Mrs May, was a proponent of a hard form of Brexit to which a majority of MPs were opposed. By this stage, negotiations with the EU were at a critical juncture and MPs did not wish to relinquish their unusual power over the making of policy, so they would not vote for a new general election. Therefore, until a deal was done with the opposition parties in December 2019 to allow a new general election, Mr Johnson was forced to live with the recalcitrant Parliament he had inherited.

36 The Fixed Term Parliaments Act 2011.

This unfolding political picture provides the background for the two *Miller* cases in the Supreme Court.[37] I will discuss them in chapter 4.

In *Miller I* the Supreme Court held that legislative approval from Parliament was required before notice was given under article 50 of the Treaty on European Union to withdraw from the EU. In the event there proved to be little difficulty in getting the relevant legislation through Parliament.

The second *Miller* case took place when Boris Johnson was, in a certain sense, a prisoner of Parliament because of the fixed-term legislation. At a critical point in the government's negotiations with the EU on the terms of Brexit it seems he wished to be free of the risk that a majority of MPs might take action to limit his freedom of manoeuvre in those negotiations.

Johnson asked the Queen to prorogue Parliament for a period of five weeks at this critical juncture. In its judgment in *Miller II* the Supreme Court held that the prorogation was unlawful. This judgment, like that in *Miller I*, sought to uphold the authority of Parliament against the claims of the executive to be able to rule without reference to it.

However, again, this had little political impact. The reasons for this lie in the way in which the British constitution is fashioned around the executive as the active ingredient. It is the executive, through its party organisation and control of business in Parliament, which proposes policy programmes and initiates legislation to implement them. Outside those structures, MPs are not well-positioned to assume the initiative themselves. They proved to be incapable of forming a cross-party alliance to stop the government's negotiation position from being carried through.

The final denouement was the December 2019 general election. In a political miscalculation, the opposition parties agreed to vote for this election ahead of time. The Conservatives under Mr Johnson won a decisive 80-seat majority on their programme to 'Get Brexit Done'.

37 *R (Miller) v Secretary of State for Exiting the European Union* [2017] UKSC 5; [2018] AC 61 ('*Miller I*') and *R (Miller) v Prime Minister* [2019] UKSC 41; [2020] AC 373 ('*Miller II*').

In political terms this election restored the functioning of the constitution around its traditional fundamental principles. The Brexit outcome from the application of the alien principle of direct democracy in the referendum has been brought back into alignment with a Brexit outcome secured in conventional means in a general election pursuant to the traditional principle of representative democracy. By legislation passed by the new government the Act fixing a set term for Parliament was repealed in 2022.[38]

Political and Legal Constraints on the Agency of Parliament

There are further political constraints on the agency of Parliament. There are also legal constraints upon it.

(i) Political Constraints

To take the political constraints first, I would highlight four.

First, as mentioned in chapter 2, there is a mismatch between the increased need for positive law in modern society and the essentially fixed capacity of the House of Commons to deal with business. Its size has not grown significantly since the nineteenth century, and it has not significantly modified its procedures for enacting primary legislation to enable it to do more. As the demands on Parliament have increased, its relative capacity to exercise its own agency in dealing with them has been eroded. The practical effects of this have been to place a high premium on parliamentary time, as a scarce resource, and to foster the growth in the use of subordinate legislation by ministers, with minimal scrutiny in Parliament, as described in chapter 2. This means that a great deal of legislation is being created without substantive exercise of judgment by Parliament itself.

38 By the Dissolution and Calling of Parliament Act 2022.

Second, the Burkean model of deliberative democracy has come under enormous strain. This was a model for the exercise of considered judgment by Parliament itself as a collectivity. It is this model which is at the heart of Jeremy Waldron's argument for upholding the dignity of legislation based on a rather idealised view of deliberative democracy in Parliament.[39] Now it is comparatively rare for MPs to engage in substantive deliberation with each other in the chamber in holding the government to account or before legislating. An aggregative model of democracy has become predominant, based on party loyalty.

Nevil Johnson writes that 'the rise of disciplined political parties, often claiming a mandate to act by virtue of an electoral majority, has introduced a profound ambiguity into the relationship between Parliament and the government. Is the House of Commons there to confer authority on the executive and to exercise a critical and controlling function in relation to its members, or is its main function now to facilitate majority rule and the fulfilment of promises made by parties in an election?'[40] According to Johnson, Burke's theory of representative democracy, with loose political parties and an emphasis on policy formed through debate, is all but dead; there has been a shift 'away from an idea of representation emphasising the independence of judgment expected of the representative and towards acceptance of the primacy of party ties in the competition for electoral support'.[41] Political parties offer programmes to the electorate, reduced to simple promises, and careers to their candidates: 'It is on this essentially populist foundation that parliamentary government in Britain has assumed the character of "mandated majoritarian government" or . . . "majoritarian democracy"'.[42] Further, such has been the expansion of the governance function that Parliament no longer has the capacity for continuous supervision of the executive.[43]

39 J. Waldron, *Law and Disagreement* (1999) and *The Dignity of Legislation* (1999). Waldron treats the passing of Abortion Act 1967 as a prime example of the parliamentary process, whereas it is atypical.

40 N. Johnson, *Reshaping*, 104.

41 Ibid, 293.

42 Ibid, 290–291.

43 Ibid, 312.

These changes are associated with profound underlying changes in the nature of the state. Johnson points to a big shift in expectations as to the role of the state since Dicey's time, which has put pressure on the workings of the constitution. He characterises this in terms of the rise and fall of negative liberty (hostility to extensive public powers, so that as far as possible people should be free to do what they like), which ran into difficulties in the transition from a negative laissez-faire state to one committed to the promotion of economic and social welfare.[44] This has been associated with a change in the role of the central government and the terms of party competition. Traditions of institutional pluralism and powers diffused to local self-governing councils have been eroded as parties compete on national platforms to acquire and then use centralised state power.[45] There has been increased emphasis on the implementation of uniform nation-wide standards of service provision. The driving force in a shift away from nineteenth-century traditions of pluralism and subsidiarity has been the urge of national party leaderships to extend their capacity to meet the expectations of the electorate, with a corresponding weakening of political leverage available to groups at local levels.[46] The power of the executive, operating within Parliament and making use of the supremacy of Parliament, 'is largely free from the checks and balances imposed by the need to accommodate the constitutionally recognised rights of competing institutions within the political system'.[47]

Johnson's diagnosis may be overly pessimistic, in that there does remain scope for deliberation in Parliament, at least sometimes. The recent debate about the law on assisted dying is an example, albeit it is not typical. The Waldron vision of the dignity of legislation is under pressure, but it is not entirely defunct. Also, the power which the executive possesses is dependent on their ability to exercise control through Parliament. MPs can vote to remove a government on a vote of confidence, so the executive has to behave in a way which keeps a sufficient number content so

44 Ibid, ch 2.
45 Ibid, ch 3 and see chapter 2.
46 Ibid, 50–51.
47 Ibid, ch 5, 98.

as to avoid that. Also, parliamentarians can slow down or reject proposed legislation. The ability to slow down the legislative process is itself a potentially powerful lever in their hands to bargain for changes in Bills, because parliamentary time is a scarce resource which has to be spent carefully by any government with a crowded legislative programme. It follows that much of the practical agency exercised by parliamentarians occurs behind the scenes, with bargaining conducted internally through party structures and then across the aisle.

However, Johnson's diagnosis sets the scene for challenges which any constitution of a modern state has to face: the integration of popular will with respect for individual rights, effective and appropriate control of the exercise of executive discretion and the delivery of services, and maintenance of appropriate levels of subsidiarity for popular decision-making. The problems may be particularly acute for the UK constitution, since, according to Johnson, party interest in the acquisition and retention of power has steadily eroded norms of self-restraint by office-holders and a sense of limits of powers which is integral to liberal constitutional ideology; and the interests of the party are given priority over the public interest, so institutional practices of restraint are in a state of decay.[48] Already in the 1920s, Carl Schmitt called attention to the erosion of parliamentary deliberative democracy under the impact of mass party politics in his book *The Crisis of Parliamentary Democracy*.[49] The erosion of customary political norms of self-restraint means that there is pressure for law to take the strain and fill in gaps where the nineteenth-century forms of government do not meet current needs. I will come back to this topic in chapter 4.

At the most fundamental level, the question arises of the extent to which the principle of parliamentary sovereignty in its unconstrained form is ultimately predicated on a perception that the political constraints on the exercise of power are effective to prevent potentially tyrannical abuse. David Feldman discusses this issue in his recent book, *Key*

48 Ibid, 16. See also L. Siedentop, *Democracy in Europe* (2001), chs 4–6.

49 C. Schmitt, *The Crisis of Parliamentary Democracy* (2nd ed [1926], trans E. Kennedy, MIT Press, 1985).

Ideas in Constitutional Law.[50] He observes that 'relying on the moderation and shared ethical sense of political elites becomes less safe in times of extremist beliefs and populist politics unmoderated by common backgrounds, upbringing, education and respect for objective truth, expertise and elites', and that we have departed from the shared ethos of an aristocratic tradition in government 'which made the theory of a legally unfettered legislature acceptable in a freedom-respecting society'.[51] Anxiety about the views of the electorate at the next election operates as another and different sort of constraint on the executive, but this could be perceived as giving rise to the possibility of the tyranny of the majority in a particularly raw form.

Another perspective from which the doctrine of parliamentary sovereignty may be questioned is the transformation of party politics from the relatively loose party arrangements in the nineteenth century to a much tighter and more disciplined form in the twentieth and twenty-first centuries. The concept of parliamentary sovereignty was fed by the Burkean idea that Parliament was a site for reasoned and reflective consideration of the common good by parliamentarians, according to their own best judgment. In other words, it was a concept well suited to give concrete effect to a deliberative form of democracy. But stricter party discipline has eroded the scope for the individual exercise of judgment by parliamentarians.[52]

From both these perspectives it could be argued that whereas the concept of parliamentary sovereignty reflected and was justified by forms

50 D. Feldman, *Key Ideas in Constitutional Law* (2025), 83–91.

51 Ibid, 87.

52 According to Carl Schmitt's analysis in *The Crisis of Parliamentary Democracy*, the legitimacy of parliamentary democracy, arising from the deliberative form of democracy available through debate by representatives in the legislature, was undermined by direct political engagement with the people through political parties aiming to secure their engagement in new forms of mass politics which had developed by the twentieth century. There is some echo of this in political developments in the UK: in order to secure electoral success, national parties have to devise national programmes to appeal to the electorate, to be carried through by MPs who are dependably loyal to the party line—although, as mentioned above, there does remain scope for deliberation in Parliament, including by negotiation within parties.

of political practice prevalent in the nineteenth century—the time at which it received its canonical formulation by Dicey—there is now a mismatch between that concept and the current forms of political practice. However, the other significant change which has occurred is the growing force of democratic ideology throughout the nineteenth and twentieth centuries. This has to a degree underpinned these changes in political practice, as national parties have grown up to compete for support from a national electorate of equal citizens.

Therefore, given the strength of the tradition of parliamentary sovereignty, its alignment with democratic ideology, and the absence of a written constitution setting out positive legal rules to set against it, it is difficult for a court to locate in clear terms whether and when the principle of parliamentary sovereignty might reach a limit. Nevil Johnson points out that the ideal of parliamentary government combines with the first past the post electoral system still to connect voters to rulers, through the key ability of the electorate to get rid of a government in an election.[53] This remains the basis for popular acceptance of the regime. 'In the British constitutional tradition . . . the principle of parliamentary sovereignty really became another way of talking about the sovereignty of the people, democracy and self-government'.[54] This is why the idea of Parliament and its unlimited authority has been so powerful in the popular imagination: 'it has stood for democratic self-government and for the affirmation that all executive authority is held in trust and that those exercising it must be publicly accountable to representatives of the people', in a form of 'fusion of parliamentary and popular sovereignty'.[55] This aspect of the UK constitution is fundamental to the respect for parliamentary sovereignty, which is the basis for the agency which Parliament continues to have.[56]

53 Johnson, *Reshaping*, 292.

54 Ibid, 292.

55 Ibid, 31.

56 See also Lord Bingham of Cornhill, 'The Rule of Law and the Sovereignty of Parliament' (2008) 19 *King's Law Journal* 223.

Moreover, public respect for Parliament means that it exercises agency through being the site for authoritative resolution of conflicts of interest and conflicts of view between different groups in society. Political conflict is such that aggregative democracy (giving outcomes by the counting of votes) is ultimately necessary to provide binding decisions, as the channel for social forces to be recognised and accommodated peacefully under generally accepted conditions. Indeed, recognition that one side has been defeated in a vote on an issue may be the best way of demonstrating respect for them in the political process, rather than in a pretence of a false deliberative unanimity.[57] To be viable as a legitimate mode of governance, however, aggregative democracy requires a basic level of loyalty to the constitution from the losers on a particular issue or in a particular election, so that they will keep playing the game and accept its outcomes rather than overturn the board.

Both the deliberative and the aggregative conceptions of democracy highlight an important feature of the political realm which the legal realm cannot replicate, namely the scope it provides for compromise and negotiation in relation to competing interests. Outcomes arrived at through political compromise can accommodate many competing points of view.[58] The courts should be prepared to give effect to the legislative product of such compromises, recognising that it may not reflect any single articulated principle and without seeking to impose their own, inconsistent solutions through interpretation. The doctrine of parliamentary sovereignty ensures that this is done.

The third political constraint on the agency of Parliament is the rise of populist modes of politics. Brexit is a case in point. In one sense populism is the essence of democracy, since democracy is government according to the popular will. But as Kelsen pointed out, questions arise about how the popular will is to be identified and constituted. As Jan-Werner Müller pithily observes,[59] the essence of democracy is that the majority have their

57 B. Williams, *In the Beginning was the Deed* (2005), 13.
58 See, e.g., B. Crick, *In Defence of Politics*, 5th ed (2000).
59 J-W. Müller, *Democracy Rules* (2021), 65.

way after the minority have their say: that is, majority rule is valid, but there should be respect for, and a hearing of, minority opinions.

In a remark aimed at Rousseau and his conception of the general will, Hannah Arendt said that the political world is framed by and created for 'men' (and of course, women), not 'Man' with a capital 'M'. Her point was that politics has to accommodate a plurality of views and values.[60] It is dangerous to suppress this perspective by compressing humans, with all their individuality, into one theoretical homogenised whole.

For modern democratic polities, the fundamental political theory of sovereignty is that it is the people who are sovereign. In our system, as Dicey observed, this theory applies, but alongside it sits the legal principle of the sovereignty of Parliament. We have a representative parliamentary democracy. This juxtaposition of a political theory of popular sovereignty and a legal theory of parliamentary sovereignty is capable of giving rise to tensions. Indeed, it did so during the Brexit saga, after the 2016 referendum result gave a concrete answer to a question addressed to the people themselves.

The idea that the people are sovereign opens up powerful rhetorical possibilities for political debate with a view to assembling political forces outside and within Parliament: if opponents can be portrayed as defying the will of the people, that is not a good look in a democracy.

Experimentation with direct democracy in the form of referendums, involving a direct appeal to 'the people' to state their will by voting on some proposal, reinforces this possibility. The mantra of 'Get Brexit done' illustrated this. Some politicians were able to leverage the Brexit referendum result to promote outcomes they desired, and others found it difficult to resist that rhetorical appeal.

Another set of tensions is created by the second pillar of the constitution identified by Dicey, the rule of law. This is a rather ambiguous idea. It can be read as a relatively thin conception, in the sense that law, however it is properly to be identified, has to be obeyed, including by

60 H. Arendt, *The Human Condition* (1959), 9 ("Men, not Man, live on the earth and inhabit the world").

the government. But it can also be read more extensively and given greater substantive meaning. The more that happens, the more the meaning and effect of this principle are contested. The more substantive content is given to the principle of the rule of law, the more a tension appears to arise with the popular will as expressed by Parliament through the medium of legislation. I will return to this topic in chapter 4.

In thinking about the scope for populism in our legal system both these boundaries are significant. First, there is the boundary between representative democracy in Parliament and the notion of the will of the people, as direct democracy, linking 'the people' and political outcomes. Second, there is the boundary between the popular will expressed through Parliament and the rule of law.

To complete the picture, one also has to understand the power of the executive in the political system, which I emphasised in chapter 2. Usually, the executive with a majority is able to work *through* Parliament, not in opposition to it. It uses Parliament as an instrument of rule. In an important sense, therefore, Lord Hailsham's description of our political system as an elective dictatorship[61] carries force. Despite the pejorative language, this is not necessarily bad. Democracy would be discredited if elected politicians could not do effectively what they have promised the electorate they will do. But where should the limits lie?

Jan-Werner Müller explains:[62]

> Populism arises with the introduction of representative democracy; it is its shadow. Populists hanker after ... 'holism': the notion that the polity should no longer be split and the idea that it's possible for the people to be one and – all of them – to have one true representative. The core claim of populism is thus a moralized form of anti-pluralism. . . . Populism requires a *pars pro toto* argument and a claim to exclusive representation, with both understood in a moral, as opposed to empirical, sense. There can be no populism, in other words, without someone speaking in the name of the people as a whole.

61 Lord Hailsham, the 5th Richard Dimbleby Lecture, 9 October 1976.
62 J-W. Müller, *What is Populism?* (2016), 20.

To make such a claim is a rhetorical move in the political realm to silence debate, with the aim of generating political power and, consequent on that, legal authority. It can be a move designed to suppress the agency of Parliament, by eliminating the scope for genuine consideration and creating a fear of an electorate in which the possibilities for open debate appear to be much reduced.

Around the world, populism is typically framed as anti-elite and expresses impatience with institutional constraints. It maximises political claims and is dismissive of impediments to their realisation. Populist politicians promise instant, radical change. Then when it proves difficult to realise those aims in power, they need to be able to butt up against opponents whom they can blame for betraying the will of the people. Populism promotes popular as opposed to parliamentary sovereignty, and it is antagonistic.

Since the nineteenth century there has been a decline in the institutional constraint posed by Parliament on the exercise of power. Under the pressure of mass democracy and the recruitment of political support for national party programmes, there has also been an erosion of norms of political morality, which Dicey identified as a third pillar of the constitution. Despite some attempts to shore up those norms by the creation of independent regulatory guarantor institutions as described in chapter 2, these developments mean that the courts are left more exposed as defenders of the constitutional order. The *Miller II* prorogation case could be seen as a symptom of this.

So each pillar of Dicey's account of the constitution—sovereignty of Parliament, rule of law and the role of conventions—comes under pressure from populism.

There is considerable scope for populist rhetoric in the UK's political system. Perhaps the greatest risk is in relation to claims by the executive to be speaking for 'the people', when using their considerable power within Parliament and their considerable legal powers outside Parliament.[63] When the executive frames itself as the representative of

63 This is examined in A. Young, *Unchecked Power? How Recent Constitutional Reforms Are Threatening UK Democracy* (2024).

'the people', in opposition to Parliament and other institutions such as the courts, it risks the devaluation of institutions intended to secure the representation of all.

The fourth constraint on Parliament's constitutional agency is the devolution of important aspects of government to the constituent parts of the UK: the Scottish Parliament, the Northern Ireland Assembly and the Welsh Senedd. This is not a fully federal system, as there is no Assembly for England. The UK Parliament governs for England and has reserve powers in relation to the other nations. Even where matters are not reserved to the UK Parliament under the relevant devolution legislation, the UK Parliament retains the power to legislate in the area of devolved matters, as a function of the principle of parliamentary sovereignty. However, the devolved executives and the devolved assemblies have claims to democratic legitimacy for their nations, both as against the UK Parliament and as against the UK executive, which is elected predominantly on English votes and has a particular focus on England. Brexit has put pressure on the devolution settlement. A majority in Scotland voted Remain, and the Scottish government, Scottish Parliament and Scottish MPs have pressed for a softer form of Brexit and closer alignment with Europe.

In *Miller I* the Scottish government asked the Supreme Court to give legal effect to a constitutional convention known as the Sewel convention that the UK government would not legislate on a matter affecting Scotland without first seeking to secure the agreement of the Scottish government. The Court rejected this argument. It again drew on established constitutional traditions derived from Dicey's schema to hold that the convention was a matter of custom and practice which did not have legal force.

In a later case, the Scottish government tested the limits of the powers of the Scottish Parliament under the Scotland Act 1998 to influence or veto the legal rules to be put in place by the UK Parliament to give effect to the Brexit deal between the UK and the EU, in the *Continuity Bill* case.[64] The Scotland Act 1998 preserves the principle of the sovereignty

64 *In re UK Withdrawal from the European Union (Legal Continuity) (Scotland) Bill* [2018] UKSC 64; [2019] AC 1022.

of the UK Parliament, so the Supreme Court found that the Scottish Parliament lacked the power to affect the legislation of the UK Parliament on this issue. And in the *Indyref 2* decision[65] the Supreme Court held that it was not within the competence granted to the Scottish Parliament by the Scotland Act 1998 to legislate for an advisory second referendum on Scottish independence, since this was designed to put political pressure on the UK Parliament and would undermine its agency in relation to deciding whether to take any action on this topic.

So Brexit has placed the constitution of the UK under pressure. But it has been found possible ultimately to secure the basic constitutional principles of representative democracy and the sovereignty of parliament.

(ii) Legal Constraints and the Concept of Legislative Intention

Finally, I turn to consider the legal constraints regarding how Parliament exercises its agency. I will discuss these in further detail in chapter 4. The setting for that discussion has to be an account of the centrality of Parliament's agency to act to change the law in the UK's constitution. That agency, vested in Parliament, has implications for the way in which the courts should approach the interpretation of statutes.

The constitution vests in Parliament the authority to make and change law by means of statutes. Interpretation of a statute involves courts and subjects of the law understanding how that authority has been exercised. This requires them to ascertain how Parliament intended to change the law by issuing the statute in question. They have to infer from the text, context and indications of the purpose of the statute what was the precise intention of Parliament as to how the law was to be changed.

Although some commentators maintain that legislative intention is an unhelpful fiction,[66] I contend that it is in fact real and is the proper focus

65 *Reference by the Lord Advocate of devolution issues under paragraph 34 of Schedule 6 to the Scotland Act 1998* [2022] UKSC 31.

66 See e.g. A. Burrows, *Thinking about Statutes: Interpretation, Interaction, Improvement* (2018), ch 1; J. Manning, "Without the Pretense of Legislative Intent" (2017) 130 *Harvard Law Review* 2397; K. Hayne, "Statutes, Intentions and the Courts: What

for inquiry when a statute falls to be interpreted and applied.[67] The question has to be, what did Parliament mean (that is, what meaning did it intend to convey) by using the language it chose in enacting the statute? Legislative intention is a concept directly drawn from the fact that the legislature has authority to change the law and is to be taken to do so for good reasons. The legislature exercises agency, forming and acting on intentions to change the law for those reasons and to convey some particular meaning content to the subjects of the law, which it does despite the fact that it is composed of a large number of individuals, each with their own states of mind.[68]

Legislative intention has to be the focus of the interpretive exercise, even if interpretive practice may be fleshed out and stabilised to some degree by caselaw and sometimes by prior declarations by the legislature as to how its enactments are to be read.[69] The relevant inference about the meaning Parliament intended to convey is informed by the context in which it passes legislation, including what it is to be taken to know about the interpretive approaches which will be adopted by those reading it.

The determinate meaning to be given to a statute in any particular case thus depends on the intersection between two sets of practices: the legislative practice whereby a statutory text is created and the interpretive practice, as reasonably to be anticipated by the legislature, according to which it will be read, particularly by the courts.

It is true that the intention of the legislature is in a certain sense a fiction. The legislature is not a human person, but it is an artificial person—an agent. It is that artificial person which has the authority and hence the agency to act to change the law by legislating. But this is not an impediment to the use of the notion of legislative intention.

Place Does the Notion of Intention (Legislative or Parliamentary) Have in Statutory Construction?" (2013) 13 *Oxford University Commonwealth Law Journal* 271.

67 I defend this view at greater length in P. Sales, 'In Defence of Legislative Intention' (2019) 48 *Australian Bar Review* 6.

68 I find the account given in R. Ekins, *The Nature of Legislative Intent* (2012) persuasive on this.

69 As in, e.g., the Interpretation Act 1978 and according to section 3 of the Human Rights Act 1998.

Also, one is not concerned with the actual, subjective intentions of individual legislators, that is, what they meant or hoped to achieve by voting to adopt a particular legislative provision. Their actual intentions do not govern the meaning of what is jointly agreed as a text, after using defined procedures to produce one authoritative statement of law from many, often conflicting, views, purposes and priorities. So, again, and as an aspect of the first point, one has to treat the legislature as an artificial person. But this also does not disqualify the notion of legislative intention from having a role in working out the meaning of a statute. It simply means that the intention is that of the artificial person which is the legislature, to be determined objectively according to the inferences to be drawn as a result of consideration of the two sets of practices referred to. Indeed, working out what the legislature intended by using the words it chose in the context in which it was legislating is the object of statutory interpretation, since this is how the agency granted to it by the constitution is respected.

By these means the democratic will is identified in precise legal form by being developed by a process of crystallisation, starting from formation of public opinion in the wider political environment through more procedural filters of parliamentary deliberation, to the production of a single binding statement of policy in the legal form of a statute.

The basic issue revolves around deriving a coherent view of public policy, as ultimately expressed authoritatively in an act of legislation, from a plurality of human beings. The concept of legislative intention provides normative coherence which is essential to promote constitutional values. The legislative will is the will of the people, in refined and concretised form.

The legislature clearly does exercise agency. It acts deliberately and on the basis of reasons to change the law in specific ways and to further specific objectives. I suggest that the notion of legislative intention is the concept which is appropriate to capture this constitutional and indeed factual reality. It is not incoherent or indefensible. It is constitutionally and logically necessary. It simply reflects the agency which the legislature undoubtedly exercises.

The legislature exercises agency and uses language on a collective, co-operative basis. The co-operation is founded on the use of language and the mutual reliance of parliamentarians that the texts on which they vote can and will be read in ways which they understand will give effect to their collectively chosen objectives. Fair notice to parliamentarians of the meaning of such texts, relying on generally accepted rules of grammar and meaning, as located in the specific legislative context, promotes equality of voice and vote when they act together and is a necessary foundation for the coherent expression of collective agency. This perspective, internal to the legislature, is not always brought out clearly in commentaries. An objective approach to identifying legislative intention and the meaning of statutes is necessary, both as the foundation for the coherent exercise of legislative will by parliamentarians in the first place and for rule of law reasons. These relate to the virtues of predictability of application of laws for those subject to them and giving fair notice of the legal requirements being imposed upon them.

As Richard Ekins writes: 'the legal meaning of a statutory text is the meaning one infers the legislature intended to convey in uttering the semantic content of the text in the particular context of the enactment'; this 'involves and informs inference about the reasoned choice or choices that explain the enactment'; and 'the meaning of the statutory text is to be found by reasoning about what meaning was likely intended by the legislature that actually enacted that text'.[70]

Joseph Raz puts it this way:[71]

> To give a person or an institution law-making powers is to entrust them with the power to make law by acts intended to make law, or at least undertaken in the knowledge that they make law. It makes no sense to give any person or body law-making power unless it is assumed that the law they make is the law they intended to make.

70 R. Ekins, "Statutes, Intentions and the Legislature: A Reply to Justice Hayne" (2014) 14 *Oxford University Commonwealth Law Journal* 3, 6.

71 J. Raz, "Intention in Interpretation" in *The Autonomy of Law: Essays on Legal Positivism* (1996), 258.

Raz considers that a joint intention of legislators can be identified. He therefore takes issue with two other prominent philosophers, Ronald Dworkin and Jeremy Waldron, who rely upon the multi-member nature of legislatures to contend that there is no such thing as legislative intention.[72]

John Gardner makes similar points to Raz.[73] Legislated law is intentionally made. Parliament does intend to change the law. All parliamentarians who participate in legislative activity, including those on the losing side of any vote, intend to participate in doing that. As Gardner puts it: 'An agent acts intentionally inasmuch as it does what it does for (what it takes to be) reasons'.[74] Clearly, reasons are given for and against changing the law. That is indeed the purpose of legislative debate, and behind that it is the purpose of wider public debate about policy and law, and ultimately may be the purpose of holding a general election in which the public will can be tested. Legislation is the act of one agent, and that agent may be an institution such as Parliament. Gardner explains that there is nothing wrong with the idea of concerted agency, for there are artificial concerted agents, and many are creatures of the law. He writes:

> It does not follow from the fact that they are creatures of the law that they do not exist or that they are not agents. On the contrary, it follows from the fact that they can perform actions with legal effect, such as legislating, that they do exist and that they are agents.[75]

Since Parliament is an agent formed for the purpose of making decisions about what the law should be, its intention in that regard is inferred from reading the statutory text as the utterance of a presumptively rational agent deciding what to do in the particular context, which is capable of acting coherently for reasons and purposes of its own.[76] Further, since those subject to the law enacted by Parliament reasonably expect the

72 Ibid, 264–265. Cf R. Dworkin, *Law's Empire* (1986), 336; J. Waldron, *Law and Disagreement* (1999), 43.
73 J. Gardner, "Some Types of Law", ch 2 in D. Edlin (ed), *Common Law Theory* (2007).
74 Ibid, 57.
75 Ibid, 59–60.
76 As Richard Ekins cogently argues.

lawgiver to act as a rational agent, that is how they interpret the statutes enacted by it; so it is a matter of basic fairness to them that the courts should adopt the same approach to interpretation.

This is the theoretical underpinning for what is the orthodox and long-established doctrinal position in English law. In 1877, Lord Blackburn said in the *River Wear Commissioners* case[77] that the principles applicable to construing a statute were the same as those for construing other instruments in writing:

> In all cases the object is to see what is the intention expressed by the words used. But, from the imperfection of language, it is impossible to know what that intention is without inquiring farther, and seeing what the circumstances were with reference to which the words were used, and what was the object, appearing from those circumstances, which the person using them had in view; for the meaning of words varies according to the circumstances with respect to which they were used.
>
> . . .
>
> The office of the Judges is not to legislate, but to declare the expressed intention of the Legislature.'

In the *Black-Clawson* case[78] Lord Reid said:

> We often say that we are looking for the intention of Parliament, but that is not quite accurate. We are seeking the meaning of the words which Parliament used. We are seeking not what Parliament meant but the true meaning of what they said.

This was a statement directed, entirely rightly, at focusing primarily on the text legislated by Parliament when looking to see how it changed the law by that text. It was not a statement intended to discredit the notion of identifying the intention of Parliament as inferred from that text as adopted in the circumstances in which Parliament legislated. Later in his speech, in addressing the meaning to be attached to the words used in the provision in question, Lord Reid reasoned that no good draftsman

77 *River Wear Commissioners v Adamson* (1877) 2 App Cas 743, 763–764.
78 *Black-Clawson International Ltd v Papierwerke Waldhof-Aschaffenburg AG* [1975] AC 591, at 613.

would 'have employed such an obscure expression if the intention had been to deal with the defendant's judgments'.[79] In construing the statute Lord Reid was simply following what he described as 'The general rule in construing any document', which is 'that one should put oneself "in the shoes" of the maker or makers and take into account relevant facts known to them when the document was made'.[80] Lord Reid's approach is thus the same as that of Lord Blackburn a century before. The conclusion of the House of Lords in *Black-Clawson*, adopting this approach, was that the courts should refer to the report of a law reform commission, which had been before Parliament when it legislated, as an aid to the construction of the statute.

The speeches of the other Law Lords in *Black-Clawson* adopted essentially the same approach as Lord Blackburn and Lord Reid. Viscount Dilhorne said:

> The task confronting a court when construing a statute is to determine what was Parliament's intention. In a perfect world the language employed in the Act would not be capable of more than one interpretation but due in part to the lack of precision of the English language, often more than one interpretation is possible. Then, to enable Parliament's intention to be determined, as I understand the position, one may have regard to what was the law at the time of the enactment and to what was the mischief at which it was directed.[81]

Lord Simon of Glaisdale said:

> Courts of construction interpret statutes with a view to ascertaining the intention of Parliament expressed therein. But, as in interpretation of all written material, what is to be ascertained is the meaning of what Parliament has said and not what Parliament meant to say.[82]

He also cited Lord Blackburn's statement in the *River Weir Commissioners* case.[83]

79 At 617.
80 At 613–614.
81 At 622.
82 At 625.
83 At 627.

The courts have for a very, very long time adopted the practice of looking for guidance for the interpretation of statutes, especially when their application to particular facts is unclear or they are ambiguous, to materials from which inferences can be drawn about the likely intention of the enacting Parliament.

In *Black-Clawson* Lord Simon explained how legislative practice and interpretive practice intersect in the interpretation of statutes, as a practical way to reconcile the constitutional pillars of the sovereignty of Parliament and the rule of law:

> interpretation cannot be concerned wholly with what the promulgator of a written instrument meant by it: interpretation must also be frequently concerned with the reasonable expectation of those who may be affected thereby. This is most clearly to be seen in the interpretation of a contract: it has long been accepted that the concern of the court is not so much with the subject-matter of consent between the parties (which may, indeed, exceptionally, be entirely absent) as with the reasonable expectation of the promisee. So, too, in statutory construction, the court is not solely concerned with what the citizens, through their parliamentary representatives, meant to say; it is also concerned with the reasonable expectation of those citizens who are affected by the statute, and whose understanding of the meaning of what was said is therefore relevant. The sovereignty of Parliament runs in tandem with the rule of objective law . . . if the draftsman uses the tools of his trade correctly, the meaning of his words should actually represent what their promulgator meant to say and the court of construction, retracing the same path in the opposite direction, should arrive, via the meaning of what was said, at what the promulgator meant to say.[84]

Lord Simon's statement illustrates the point that in an important sense the respect due to the rule of law is the respect due to the processes by which the law is made. Where law takes the form of statute, to give effect to the statute according to Parliament's intention, as objectively manifested by the words it has chosen to use, is precisely to give effect to Parliament's constitutional authority. Where it is the common law which is in issue, application of that law according to the common law tradition

84 [1975] AC 591, 645.

and subject to the constraints it imposes is to respect the common law processes by which it came into being and by which it may be developed.

Lord Simon's statement is also an illustration of Montesquieu's point that freedom may be protected and promoted by the separation of powers.[85] A court is an institution separate from Parliament which has to understand its legislation from an external point of view. The fact that the court interprets the law which Parliament has promulgated ensures that the reasonable expectations of citizens as to what it means are protected: they can safely rely on what Parliament appears to have said.

Through the operation of declarations about interpretive practice, the courts and Parliament have both moved to articulate or introduce significant constraints in relation to the exercise of agency by Parliament, principally in relation to individual rights.

The flagship legislation here is the Human Rights Act 1998. Section 3 enacts a strong interpretive obligation that legislation should be construed where 'possible' so as to be compatible with the Convention rights set out in the European Convention on Human Rights.[86] This means that if Parliament wishes to legislate in a manner which is inconsistent with those rights it has to do so in very clear terms, so that it is not 'possible' to read the legislation in a compatible way. There is much litigation around this boundary. The practical implication in terms of parliamentary agency is that it imposes a sort of manner and form constraint on what Parliament can do. Parliament can override the Convention rights, but it is obliged to do so by proceeding in the right way.

Where it is not possible to give legislation an interpretation under section 3 which is compatible with Convention rights, a court can issue a declaration of incompatibility under section 4. Formally in domestic law this only triggers a ministerial power, without obligation, to promulgate subordinate legislation to effect a conforming amendment of the primary legislation. The declaration does not affect the enforceability of the legislation in question according to its non-compatible meaning.

85 Montesquieu, *The Spirit of the Laws* (1748), Book 11, chapter 6; Book 19, chapter 27.
86 See *Ghaidan v Godin-Mendoza* [2004] AC 557.

However, where a declaration of incompatibility is issued, if the minister does not make an amending order, the individual affected can make an application to the European Court of Human Rights and it is likely they will succeed in obtaining a judgment against the government. A declaration of incompatibility therefore has a practical effect which is far greater than the formal effect it has under section 4. As Aileen Kavanagh points out in *The Collaborative Constitution*,[87] the government has almost always reacted to a declaration of incompatibility by changing the law to put it into a compatible form.[88]

Therefore, whilst there is no formal power of strong form judicial review in the UK to strike down primary legislation, a declaration of incompatibility comes close to having that effect in practical terms. Although it appears to be something of a paper tiger on the face of it, it is in reality a powerful remedy. It is a form of *ex post facto* constraint on the agency of Parliament, since it tends to remove practical decision-making from Parliament to the courts and the executive government. For the executive government, this is one feature of its role in managing the interface between domestic law and international law, touched on in chapter 2. It is also a form of advance constraint on Parliament, since if it wishes to pass legislation which will stand and be effective, it has to try to avoid producing something which is not compatible with Convention rights.

As I will discuss in chapter 4, the question of compatibility of legislation with Convention rights often turns on the ambit of the margin of appreciation. One aspect of the doctrine of the margin of appreciation

87 A. Kavanagh, *The Collaborative Constitution* (2024).

88 There was a saga in relation to the UK's reaction to the decision of the European Court of Human Rights decision in *Hirst v United Kingdom* (2004) 38 EHRR 40 (followed also by a declaration of incompatibility in *Smith v Scott* 2007 SC 345) that denial of voting rights for persons serving prison sentences was in breach of their Convention rights. Successive governments were opposed to changing the law in the light of this, and the relevant statutory provision has not been changed. But some administrative changes were made to soften the effect of the rule and in 2018 the Committee of Ministers supervising the UK's compliance with the judgment in *Hirst* found that enough had been done. Thus the impact of the judgment was to compel the UK government to make some changes in order to satisfy the Strasbourg enforcement mechanism. The position was recently reviewed by the European Court of Human Rights in *Hora v United Kingdom*, judgment of 23 September 2025, in which no violation was found.

is that the greater and more careful the preparation of reports for and debate in Parliament, the wider the margin tends to be and therefore the more likely it is that legislation will be found to be compatible.[89] So Parliament has the ability to buy a wider margin of appreciation for itself by proceeding in a way which demonstrates that it has paid attention to the impacts on individual rights. This is a doctrine which tends to enhance the quality of deliberation in Parliament with a view to reconciling the collective and individual interests at stake in an acceptable way.

Finally, the courts have developed domestic legal doctrine in ways that both recognise and give effect to Parliament's agency, but which also constrain it.

The courts give effect to Parliament's agency by seeking to identify, fairly and objectively, Parliament's intention as expressed in the legislation it passes. As I have mentioned, there is a very long history to this. Statutory interpretation is itself a form of constitutional law. The focus on identifying Parliament's intended meaning is a focus on recognising and respecting its agency in the constitution.

By the use of recognised canons of interpretation, the courts also constrain Parliament to some degree in the exercise of its agency. They do this through applying the principle of legality as a presumption regarding the interpretation of legislation. The principle of legality recognises a series of fundamental constitutional principles (such as that legislation does not bind the Crown) and fundamental individual rights recognised in the common law and holds that Parliament is presumed not to intend to override these principles or rights unless it makes its intention to do so very clear. As Lord Hoffmann pointed out in the *Simms* case,[90] the effect of this interpretive methodology is very similar to the operation of section 3 of the Human Rights Act 1998.[91]

89 See *Application of JR123 for Judicial Review* [2025] UKSC 8, para 58; *R (SC) v Secretary of State for Work and Pensions* [2021] UKSC 26; [2022] AC 223, paras 163–185.

90 *R v Secretary of State for the Home Department, ex p. Simms* [2000] 2 AC 115, 131–132.

91 The nature of the rights which are the interpretive reference point for this methodology is somewhat different in each case: various of the Convention rights have defeasibility built into them, typically by reference to the proportionality principle, and are thus inherently more flexible in their application than domestic fundamental rights applicable

Through the principle of legality, the common law recognises a form of presumptive constitutional order. Parliament has the power to disapply this order, but it can only do so by proceeding in the proper manner and with sufficient clarity. By an extension of this type of reasoning, certain statutes are regarded as having constitutional status so that, again, Parliament will only be capable of overriding their continued effect if it legislates in a particularly clear manner.[92]

That brings us to the most powerful illustration of the operation of the principle of legality, the question of whether there are limits on the doctrine of parliamentary sovereignty itself to prevent Parliament from having the power to remove access to the courts to challenge decisions taken by ministers or tribunals. The *Privacy International* case is now the leading authority.[93] There were dicta in the case to suggest that there might be such a limit on parliamentary sovereignty.

Two points should be made about this. First, there is no doubt that the presumption that Parliament does not intend to legislate to remove access to the courts in some shape or form is a very powerful one. This reflects the status of the rule of law as the second pillar of the constitution according to Dicey's schema.

Secondly, I am sceptical about the strength of the argument currently in the fore in support of the idea that there is a limit on parliamentary sovereignty, as opposed to a strong presumption. That argument is that it is logically inconsistent to say that Parliament passes legislation containing certain rights and that it can also legislate to prevent a person on whom those rights have been conferred from having access to the courts to enforce them.[94]

under the principle of legality, which tend to take the form of bright line rules which, if applicable, simply exclude the operation of general statutory provisions: see p. 92 below.

92 *Thoburn v Sunderland City Council* [2003] QB 151; *R (HS2 Action Alliance Ltd) v Secretary of State for Transport* [2014] UKSC 3; [2014] 1 WLR 324.

93 *R (Privacy International) v Investigatory Powers Tribunal* [2019] UKSC 22; [2020] AC 491.

94 *R (Cart) v Upper Tribunal* [2011] QB 120, paras 34–38 (Laws LJ) and *Privacy International*, para 160 (Lord Lloyd-Jones: 'it is a necessary corollary of the sovereignty of Parliament that there should exist an authoritative and independent body which can interpret and mediate legislation made by Parliament').

Something missing from this account is the fact that Parliament is not a singular entity which exists unchangingly across time. In reality and in constitutional theory there is a series of separate Parliaments, each of which is constituted differently after a general election and has a limited life span. Each Parliament exercises agency of its own. Thus, at least where there is legislation passed by one Parliament which confers rights and the question is whether the legislation passed by another Parliament is effective to prevent access to a court in some way to enforce those rights, it does not seem to me to involve logical inconsistency to say that it may do. No doubt there is a very strong principle of comity between successive Parliaments that they will not lightly undermine rights enacted by a predecessor, but that seems to support the powerful presumption I have mentioned rather than a rule which absolutely bars the later Parliament from doing this. It is an orthodox feature of parliamentary sovereignty that it is continuing and that an earlier Parliament cannot bind a later Parliament.

The same argument applies even within the life of the same Parliament. This is because it exercises its agency at different times and, as a consequence of its sovereignty, on each occasion it has full power to do whatever it wishes, according to its assessment of what the common good requires.

Conclusion

The question of the constitutional agency of Parliament is a complex one. We have to break down the concept of agency into political and legal elements. Parliament does not exercise agency itself in a full political sense. The executive is the body which does that. However, Parliament has a full power of agency in a legal sense. The basic rule of the UK constitution is parliamentary sovereignty. In the *Jackson* case Lord Bingham described this as the bedrock of the constitution.[95] Even though from

95 *R (Jackson) v Attorney General* [2005] UKHL 56; [2006] 1 AC 262, para 9.

time to time the question is raised, including in judicial dicta, whether it is subject to some limits and what they might be,[96] I think that at the very least the working hypothesis in an account of constitutional agency and constitutional principle is that parliamentary sovereignty is the rule. I will examine this further in chapter 4.

96 See the *Jackson* and *Privacy International* cases.

4

Constitutional Agency as Exercised by the Courts

Maitland wrote to Dicey, 'The only direct utility of legal history . . . lies in the lesson that each generation has an enormous power of shaping its own law.'[1]

Legitimacy is the foundation of the authority of the state and of its institutions. A primary object of a state is to maintain legitimacy as regards its citizens and an object of the institutions which comprise the state is to maintain legitimacy in the eyes of each other. In a complex and changing world there is no simple or single recipe for this. Legitimacy has various sources, and their force and the balance between them are susceptible to change.

This chapter seeks to explain how the courts exercise constitutional agency in both the senses I have been using that term, as outlined in chapter 1. They have a certain level of discretion allowed them by the constitution when articulating and applying the law. What they do in interpreting the law also has a reflexive effect on the form of the constitution itself.

1 Quoted in R. Cosgrove, *The Rule of Law: Albert Venn Dicey, Victorian Jurist* (1980), 177, and in *Council of Civil Service Unions v Minister for the Civil Service* [1985] AC 374, 417.

Constitutional Agency. Philip Sales, Oxford University Press. © Philip Sales 2026.
DOI: 10.1093/oso/9780197928370.003.0004

The Courts' Role and Their Implicit Constitutional Agency

The courts' primary function is to identify and apply the law in the course of resolving a dispute, which seems to indicate an absence of agency. But the courts develop the law interstitially through the processes of interpretation and application. In interpreting and applying legislation they exercise a degree of partnership with the legislature. This is a form of agency, albeit one which is highly constrained. In developing the common law they similarly exercise a form of agency, in that case constrained by established common law principles.

The agency which the courts exercise is both constrained and diffuse. It is constrained, because the courts operate to apply established rules and principles, and this limits their scope for action. Their agency is mediated through the principles they apply. They operate within a constitutional tradition and are subject to legal parameters. Their agency takes the form of a power to develop that tradition incrementally from within. They do not have the sort of wide powers of decision available under the constitution to the executive and to Parliament.

The application of legal norms is a constant process, which can arise in the courts at any time and in relation to any kind of case. The action of the courts is limited because it depends on the vagaries and randomness of litigation. This distinguishes it from legislative action, where the focus is on a specific act at a particular time to define new laws to govern in the future. The judicial application of an already existing norm binds together past, present and future in a way that a legislative act does not. A judge has to understand how the norm to be applied came to exist in the past and its meaning then, and decide what meaning it should bear in the present to govern the dispute before the court and (potentially) what meaning it should carry into the future to be derived from the precedential value of the decision.

The agency exercised by the courts is diffuse because it depends on which cases arise for decision and also because there are many courts making many decisions across the legal system within the framework of the constitutional tradition. Change tends to occur slowly and rather indirectly. Courts react to the cases before them. Legal reasoning is practical reasoning to deal with particular problems which present themselves on the facts. There may be a groundswell of decisions at the lower levels of the court system, responding to particular circumstances and perceived problems as they are presented in individual cases. Then at the highest level a particular change in the direction of travel may be endorsed by the apex court and encapsulated in a new authoritative statement of principle.

There are three tempos of time in a democracy embedded in a constitution framed or informed by the common law.[2] There is the need for an elected government which can respond at speed to events in the world as they unfold. This is executive time. It is characterised by a high level of discretion and flexibility for manoeuvre within very broad legal parameters. There is essentially an unavoidable need for a high degree of discretion in order to govern. A political order needs the capacity to react, and react quickly, to unpredictable changes in circumstances.

Then there is the need for the elected legislature to be able to consider proposals for reform of the law and to make decisions in light of what is judged to be the needs of the day. This is legislative time. It proceeds from public debate from which matters of public concern emerge, through refinement by application of democratic procedures (including voting in elections on the basis of party manifestos and the adoption of legislative proposals for presentation to Parliament) and onwards to enactment by Parliament as concrete laws.[3]

Finally there is the need for basic ground rules to be worked out to provide the framework for democratic contestation and engagement. This is the dimension of constitutional time in the common law tradition. In

2 For further discussion see P. Sales, 'Long Waves of Constitutional Principle', in J. Varuhas et al (eds), *The Making (and Re-Making) of Public Law* (2025).

3 See the account in J. Habermas, *Between Facts and Norms* (trans W Rehg, 1996). Of course, in emergencies the usual timing may be truncated, and use may instead be made of devices like 'sunset clauses' to ensure the legislation is brought back later for further consideration.

the dimension of constitutional time one can speak of long waves of constitutional principle in the common law. There are foundational rules which are particularly firmly embedded in the operation of the governance system so that it makes sense to speak of them as constitutional as distinct from ordinary rules of statute or the common law.

The Courts' Role in Supporting the Constitutional Agency of the Executive and Parliament: The Intention of Parliament in Legislation, the Principle of Legality and the Rationality Standard

As well as the courts exercising their own agency, the doctrines developed by them enhance the types of agency exercised by the other branches. On the one hand, in relation to the executive, by requiring legality, fairness and rationality when the executive acts the courts uphold standards of decision-making which respect underlying constitutional values and enhance the legitimacy (and therefore the overall effectiveness) of that action. By doing this the courts help the constitution as a whole to meet Bernard Williams' basic legitimation demand.[4] There is a well-known history of the development of the law of judicial review which shows the courts responding to changes in the nature of the state and the role of the executive and framing legal doctrine in the light of these.[5] On the other hand, through the development of more explicit norms in relation to the separation of powers the courts have mapped out areas where the executive is entitled to particular respect for its judgments about how to proceed. In this way they support the effectiveness of executive action, and so make another important contribution to the acceptability of the constitutional order.

4 See chapter 1.

5 See e.g. the account given by Lord Hodge in 'The Scope of Judicial Law-making in Constitutional Law and Public Law' (2021) 26 *Judicial Review* 146 and pp. 99–106 below.

In relation to Parliament, through application of the fundamental principle of parliamentary sovereignty and an approach to statutory interpretation which essentially rests upon identifying the meaning of the words chosen by Parliament in the light of the purposes pursued by Parliament,[6] the courts give effect to governance through democratic decision. At the same time, through application of the principle of legality in relation to the interpretation of legislation, the courts have identified a series of fundamental constitutional principles and rights which are treated as especially embedded and as having special status within the constitutional order so that there is a presumption that Parliament does not intend to override them. Since the articulation of legal doctrine is the province of the courts, the development of these features of statutory interpretation represents the exercise of the form of agency which resides in the courts. Particularly in relation to the principle of legality, the courts have an important role in identifying, distilling and articulating the applicable constitutional principles and rights. The courts are in this way the primary interpreters of the constitution. They also have a major role in deciding in a determinate way how the fundamental balance is to be struck between the constitutional pillars of the rule of law, including protection of individual rights, and parliamentary sovereignty. Maintaining this balance in a stable way across time is a central constitutional function.

The principle of legality has a narrow scope and is not applicable as an approach to statutory construction in the absence of a relevant established fundamental right or legally recognised constitutional principle.[7] In the *Lightfoot* case, Laws J warned that '[i]f the courts were to hold that more marginal claims of right should enjoy the protection of a rigorous rule of statutory construction not applied in contexts save that of the protection of fundamental rights and freedoms, they would impermissibly confine the powers of the elected legislature'.[8] This statement has

6 See chapter 3.
7 See e.g. *R v Secretary of State for the Home Department, ex p Stafford* [1999] 2 AC 38, 49 (Lord Steyn).
8 *R v Lord Chancellor, ex p Lightfoot* [2000] QB 597, 609.

been endorsed by the Supreme Court in *R (O) v Secretary of State for the Home Department*.[9] By treating the principle of legality with caution and keeping it within narrow bounds, the courts have made it clear that they will protect the general constitutional principle of democratic choice subject only to limited presumptive constitutional constraints. Respect for democratic legitimacy imposes an obligation on the courts to try to be clear-eyed and explicit about what background political and legal understandings really are so commonly and powerfully held as to inform statutory interpretation in this way, by application of the principle of legality; otherwise they may put their own legitimacy as decision-makers in jeopardy in the eyes of the public. This discipline has required the courts to engage in reasoning drawing on the UK's constitutional traditions to identify the constitutional rights or principles which require special recognition and protection in this way, using those traditions as a source of legitimate objective standards of judgment to which the courts can make appeal when justifying their decisions.

Parliament has exercised its own constitutional agency by laying down a general framework for the exercise by the courts of their agency as interpreters and enforcers of the law. By enactment of the Human Rights Act 1998, Parliament has given the courts an equivalent role in the interpretation of legislation under section 3 to that which they have when interpreting in accordance with the principle of legality.[10] Under section 6 it has also given the courts an enhanced role in subjecting executive action to judicial review. In both cases this has been done by setting out a table of rights to be respected, by reference to those in the European Convention on Human Rights. Section 3(1) requires the courts to interpret legislation in a way which is compatible with the Convention rights, so far as it is 'possible' to do so. Section 6(1) imposes a duty on public authorities to act in a way which is compatible with Convention rights.[11]

9 *R (O) v Secretary of State for the Home Department* [2022] UKSC 3; [2023] AC 255, para 43.

10 See chapter 3.

11 This obligation is disapplied when it conflicts with the requirements of any primary legislation which is incompatible with Convention rights and cannot be made compatible by application of the interpretive obligation under section 3(1): section 6(2). In this way,

Under this regime the courts have the role of identifying and applying the Convention rights, essentially through a process of translating them from the jurisprudence of the European Court of Human Rights in Strasbourg. In this area, again, the courts are on the front line in striking the fundamental constitutional balance between protection of individual rights and democracy, which is to say between the principles of individual autonomy and of collective self-government. Two features of that jurisprudence are particularly important in domestic constitutional terms: the margin of appreciation and an implicit sense of an appropriate allocation of powers between executive, legislature and courts in a liberal democratic state.

Through the criteria which govern the ambit of the margin of appreciation, the courts incentivise debate in Parliament and so incentivise the proper functioning of a deliberative democratic order, thereby enhancing the agency of Parliament. They also reflect the point about plural values in society and the need for resolution through the democratic process. The margin of appreciation is of particular importance in relation to the application of the proportionality doctrine as articulated by the European Court of Human Rights.[12] That doctrine states that any interference with one of the qualified or defeasible rights set out in the Convention[13] must be proportionate to a legitimate public policy objective.

Draon v France[14] provides a good example of a lower-level intensity of application of the proportionality doctrine in respect of Convention

the Human Rights Act 1998 continues to recognise and give effect to the principle of parliamentary sovereignty.

12 See P. Sales, 'The General and the Particular: Parliament and the Courts under the Scheme of the European Convention on Human Rights', ch 12 in M. Andenas and D. Fairgrieve (eds), *Tom Bingham and the Transformation of the Law* (2009); and P. Sales, 'The Developing Jurisprudence of the Supreme Court on Convention Rights' [2024] *Public Law* 444, 461–462.

13 Such as those in article 8 (respect for private and family life), article 9 (freedom of religion), article 10 (freedom of speech) and article 11 (freedom of association).

14 *Draon v France* (2006) 42 EHRR 40, paras 106–08; also see *Hatton v UK* (2003) 37 EHRR 28, para 97; *SAS v France* (2015) 60 EHRR 11, para 129.

rights in the face of recognised social disagreement and democratic resolution. The Strasbourg Court recognised that:

> the national authorities have direct democratic legitimation and are in principle better placed than an international court to evaluate local needs and conditions. In matters of general policy, on which opinions within a democratic society may reasonably differ widely, the role of the domestic policy-maker should be given special weight.

In *Animal Defenders International v UK* the Strasbourg Court attached 'considerable weight' to the fact that there had been careful consideration of its caselaw in both the parliamentary process and in the national courts as to how to strike the correct balance for article 10 purposes (freedom of speech) in the regulation of broadcasting.[15] This feature of the deliberation in the domestic political and legislative system led the Court to afford the state a widened margin of appreciation, which is to say a widened ambit of judgment within which the Court would be prepared to accept the exercise of legislative choice as compatible with the Convention rights. It was significant that the case concerned a 'general measure' in relation to which the court had to assess the legislative choices available, where '[t]he quality of the parliamentary and judicial review of the necessity of the measure is of particular importance . . . including to the operation of the relevant margin of appreciation'.[16] This may make the processes of human rights scrutiny in Parliament[17] particularly important and can be regarded as a form of incentive for the legislature to deliberate by taking the Convention rights into account when legislating.[18] Given that the central task for the constitution is to produce a stable balance between individual rights and the democratic principle, it is highly desirable that the law incentivises Parliament in this way to

15 *Animal Defenders International v UK* (2013) 57 EHRR 21.

16 Ibid, paras 106–11.

17 E.g. via the Joint Committee on Human Rights as well as in debate on the floor of the House of Commons or the House of Lords.

18 See also, in the domestic jurisprudence, *Application of JR123 for Judicial Review* [2025] UKSC 8, para 58; *R (SC) v Secretary of State for Work and Pensions* [2021] UKSC 26; [2022] AC 223, paras 163–185.

seek to strike that balance itself by having explicit regard to the individual rights and interests at stake.

As part of the principle of legality, legislation is to be construed in the light of values recognised under the common law and which it is presumed the legislature also recognises. Thus where legislation confers a discretionary power to take action against an individual there is a presumption that the power must be exercised fairly. What fairness requires depends on the context in which the power arises and the circumstances in which it falls to be exercised.[19] The open-textured nature of the fairness standard which is implied into legislation means that the courts have an active role to identify what fairness requires in any given case.

The rationality standard applied by the courts is also flexible and subject to modification depending on the particular context. The requirement that a public authority should act rationally when exercising a discretionary power is a general rule of public law. But it applies in many different contexts and the ambit of what qualifies as rational may require to be adjusted in the light of what the law recognises as particularly weighty factors which fall to be considered in a particular context. This general framework can serve both to narrow the options which are taken to be rationally open to a public authority in a particular context and to call for an enhanced level of confidence on its part (subject to careful scrutiny by the courts) that it is behaving appropriately when it acts, on the one hand, or to broaden the options available if the public authority is acting in a context where the application of political judgment and democratic accountability is at a premium. In this way the framework is responsive to the modulated application of underlying constitutional values depending on the context. Again, therefore, in the different register which applies under the rationality doctrine as compared with the principle of legality, the courts set a framework directed to maintaining a proper balance between individual rights and the principle of collective self-government.[20]

19 See e.g. *Lloyd v McMahon* [1987] AC 625; *R v Secretary of State for the Home Department, ex p. Doody* [1994] 1 AC 531.

20 See chapter 1.

The prime example of the former, narrowing approach is where an individual's human rights are in issue, where 'anxious scrutiny' (better expressed as heightened scrutiny) of a decision which interferes with those rights may be called for. The leading cases are *Bugdaycay* and *Ex parte Smith*.[21] In *Ex parte Smith*, Sir Thomas Bingham MR succinctly stated that 'the more substantial the interference with human rights, the more the court will require by way of justification before it is satisfied that the decision is rational'.[22] That is to say, the more the court will require by way of justification before it will be satisfied that the decision falls within the range of decisions which are rationally open to the public authority within the parameters of its discretion.

In certain contexts other values may be recognised in law as being of similar significance and weight so as to lead to a similar approach to the application of the rationality rule, with a corresponding narrowing of the lawful parameters of the relevant discretionary power and heightening of the scrutiny to be applied by the court. That is the position in relation to the principle that democratic engagement by councillors at the local government level should be promoted and not undermined, discussed in *Armstrong-Braun*[23] and more recently in *Spitalfields Historic Building Trust*.[24] The cases concerned the exercise of a local authority's discretionary power to make standing orders for the conduct of its business, where the standing orders had the effect of limiting in certain respects the extent to which the full council could deliberate before making a decision. Again, a form of anxious scrutiny review was applied in order

21 *R v Secretary of State for the Home Department, ex p Bugdaycay* [1987] AC 514, 531 (Lord Bridge of Harwich); *R v Secretary of State for the Home Department, ex p Brind* [1991] 1 AC 696, 748–749 (Lord Bridge) and 751 (Lord Templeman); *R v Ministry of Defence, ex p Smith* [1996] QB 517, 554–556 (Sir Thomas Bingham MR).

22 See also *R v Secretary of State for the Home Department, ex p Simms* [2000] 1 AC 115, 130 per Lord Steyn: 'the more substantial the interference with fundamental rights the more the court will require by way of justification before it can be satisfied that the interference is reasonable in a public law sense'.

23 *R v Flintshire County Council, ex p Armstrong-Braun* [2001] LGR 344, concerning the legality of a local authority's standing order to limit the circumstances in which a councillor could raise a matter for debate.

24 *R (The Spitalfields Historic Building Trust) v London Borough of Tower Hamlets* [2025] UKSC 11.

to test whether the standing orders were made within the powers of the local authority.[25]

In *R (A) v Lord Saville of Newdigate* Lord Woolf MR explained that where a fundamental right is at stake, or where a significant impact on other relevant interests is threatened, then the options available to the reasonable decision-maker are curtailed because it would be unreasonable to reach a decision which contravenes or could contravene the relevant consideration, unless there are sufficiently significant countervailing considerations.[26] In *Pham v Secretary of State for the Home Department*,[27] Lord Sumption stated: 'It is for the court to assess how broad the range of rational decision sits in the circumstances of any given case. That must necessarily depend on the significance of the right interfered with, the degree of interference involved, and notably the extent to which . . . the court is competent to reassess the balance which the decision-maker was called on to make given the subject matter'.[28] Accordingly, the rationality standard encapsulates a 'sliding scale of review, more or less intrusive according to the nature and gravity of what is at stake'.[29]

At the other end of the spectrum the range of lawful action under a discretionary power is taken to be especially wide under certain conditions, for example where the central government takes decisions in sensitive

25 As Schiemann LJ put it in *Armstrong-Braun* (para 37), the possibility that local democracy might be impeded rather than promoted by adoption of the standing order indicated that before its adoption 'the matter should be given most anxious consideration'; on the particular facts, that had not been done. In the *Spitalfields* case there had been adequate consideration.

26 [2000] 1 WLR 1855, paras 34–37. See also *R (King) v Secretary of State for Justice* [2015] UKSC 54; [2016] AC 384, para 126.

27 *Pham v Secretary of State for the Home Department* [2015] UKSC 19; [2015] 1 WLR 1591 at para 107. See also *R (Hoareau) v Secretary of State for Foreign and Commonwealth Affairs* [2020] EWCA Civ 1010; [2021] 1 WLR 472, para 155; and P. Sales, 'Rationality, Proportionality and the Development of the Law' (2013) 129 *Law Quarterly Review* 223, 226: 'depending on what is at stake (for both the interests of any individual affected by a decision and for the public interest), the margin of discretion, evaluative judgment or appreciation allowed to a public authority under both [the rationality and the proportionality] standards may be treated as narrowed or widened'.

28 See also *Spitalfields* [2025] UKSC 11, para 54.

29 *R (Begbie) v Department for Education and Employment* [2000] 1 WLR 115, para 78 (Laws LJ).

areas of social or economic policy or in the 'macro-political field'.[30] The leading authority is *R v Secretary of State for the Environment, ex p Hammersmith and Fulham London Borough Council*, which concerned central government powers to cap the amount which a local authority could charge residents by way of local taxes in the form of the community charge. Lord Bridge said that 'the formulation and the implementation of national economic policy are matters depending essentially on political judgment', and thus such decisions are not open to challenge on grounds of irrationality 'short of the extremes of bad faith, improper motive or manifest absurdity.'[31] This approach serves an important constitutional function by preserving democratic accountability for political decisions whilst protecting the legitimacy of judicial intervention by reserving it to clear cases where it is warranted. It prevents courts from being drawn into political controversies where their expertise and constitutional authority to make relevant judgments are limited. It thus supports both the exercise of agency by the executive and by the courts, by widening the scope of lawful action in the first case and by maintaining public confidence in judicial independence and impartiality which makes intervention by courts acceptable in cases when it is appropriate.

Another example of light touch review is in relation to the decision by a public authority to enter into, exercise rights under or terminate commercial contracts.[32] In *Mercury Energy* the Privy Council stated: 'It does not seem likely that a decision by a state enterprise to enter into or determine a commercial contract to supply goods or services will ever be the subject of judicial review in the absence of fraud, corruption or bad faith'.[33] As observed in *CT Power*, this limited scope for a judicial

30 For 'macro-political field', see *Begbie*, para 82 (Laws LJ). The case concerned the circumstances in which a public authority would be entitled to depart from a legitimate expectation which it had created.

31 *R v Secretary of State for the Environment, ex p Hammersmith and Fulham LBC* [1991] 1 AC 521, 594–598. See also *R (Rotherham MBC) v Secretary of State for Business, Innovation and Skills* [2015] UKSC 6, paras 21–24.

32 See *Mercury Energy Ltd v Electricity Corporation of New Zealand Ltd* [1994] 1 WLR 521; *State of Mauritius v CT Power Ltd* [2019] UKPC 27.

33 [1994] 1 WLR 521, 529.

review challenge reflects the width of the relevant discretion enjoyed by a public authority when exercising its powers to negotiate a commercial contract or to make use of its rights under such a contract.[34] Where a public body is given powers to enter into commercial contracts the ordinary implication is that it is permitted to participate in the market in the usual way, that is through the exercise of the full bargaining power available to it in order to secure the best commercial deal possible and thereby promote the public interest. Therefore, a court will be careful to ensure that application of public law standards in relation to the public body does not unduly cut down or undermine that bargaining power. Public law standards will not be applied in such a way as to give a contracting counterparty a negotiating advantage which has not been bargained for.[35]

By applying this differentiated intensity of scrutiny the courts identify and give effect to underlying constitutional rights and principles under the rubric of rationality review, as well as under the rubric of the principle of legality. But the analysis to be applied and the legal effects are different in the two cases. Broadly speaking, where the principle of legality applies in the exercise of statutory interpretation, a statutory provision cast in general terms may be wholly inapplicable. There is a bright-line barrier which prevents the executive from taking action involving interference with a constitutional right. But even if the principle of legality does not apply, so there is lawful scope for the executive to act in the exercise of its discretion, constitutional values still may apply to modify the application of the rationality standard on a sliding scale. This involves the application of a flexible standard of assessment rather than a bright-line rule. This doctrinal position allows the courts to effect a balance between constitutional rights and decision-making by democratically accountable organs in a more modulated way. The principle of legality, by contrast, is focused very precisely on the meaning and effect of a specific statutory text.

34 [2019] UKPC 27, para 66.
35 *CT Power Ltd* [2019] UKPC 27, para 63.

There is a significant gap between the operation of the principle of legality and the doctrine of anxious (or heightened) scrutiny. To achieve an effect under the principle of legality to modify what is otherwise the ordinary interpretation of a statutory provision according to the natural meaning of the words used in it, a very powerful normative impulse is required. The question is, what legitimates a court in giving what is in substance an amended meaning to the words of a statute? Key points in assessing this are that (a) for basic constitutional reasons a court is required to respect the choices made by Parliament as expressed in the language chosen by it; (b) judges do not have authority to legislate as they see fit to regulate some topic; and (c) judges have to be conscious that what they do takes place under the public gaze, so that, in order to gain public acceptance for what they do and for their role in upholding the rule of law, they have to demonstrate clearly that they have applied objective and defensible criteria when finding that the principle of legality is engaged to modify what might otherwise appear to be the ordinary meaning of a statutory provision.

In the context of the UK's democratic polity, the ultimate justification for the principle of legality is that it is a tool to identify accurately what was the intention of Parliament in enacting a statute using the language it chose in the particular context.[36] Lord Dyson MR aptly summarised its effect: 'the principle of legality is an important tool of statutory interpretation. But it is no more than that. When an issue of statutory interpretation arises, ultimately the question for the court is always to decide what Parliament intended.'[37]

The fact that the object is to ascertain the true intention of Parliament as the basis for the interpretation of legislation imposes an important discipline on the courts. The principle of legality will only be engaged by a right or principle which is established and fundamental. The principle

36 See P. Sales, 'A Comparison of the Principle of Legality and Section 3 of the Human Rights Act' (2009) 125 *Law Quarterly Review* 598.

37 *AJA v Commissioner of Police for the Metropolis* [2013] EWCA Civ 1342; [2014] 1 All ER 882, para 28.

will not apply in relation to 'more marginal claims of right'.[38] The courts are not free to impose new rights, values or principles as they see fit. Their task in determining and adhering to legislative intent is to identify rights, values and principles which are so well established that the inference can fairly be drawn that Parliament legislated with them in mind.[39]

For the principle of legality to apply, four related conditions should be fulfilled: (a) there is the relevant presence, and close normative proximity of, a constitutional value, which may be framed in terms of a fundamental or constitutional right requiring recognition, or some other constitutional principle of significance (of which there is a range);[40] (b) the constitutional principle must be one which is so clear as to be taken to be recognised by Parliament itself, so that it is plausible to infer that Parliament legislated on the unspoken assumption that the statute was to be taken to be modified by the principle (i.e. according to the basic theory underlying the principle of legality); (c) the constitutional right or principle must be identified according to reasonably objective criteria to which courts can appeal to justify invoking the principle in their interpretation of the statute; and (d) the modification of the ordinary meaning of a statute—that is of the text of a statute—must be plausible and articulated in a way which demonstrates the court's recognition of the key points referred to above.[41] Even where those conditions might otherwise be fulfilled, the expression of Parliament's intention to override the interests protected by the principle of legality might be so clearly expressed as to disqualify modification of the meaning of the provision by reference to it.[42]

38 See *R (O) v Secretary of State for the Home Department* [2022] UKSC 3; [2023] AC 255, paras 33, 36 and 43 per Lord Hodge, citing with approval the judgment of Laws J in *R (Lightfoot) v Lord Chancellor* [2000] QB 597, 609.

39 P. Sales, 'Rights and Fundamental Rights in English Law' [2016] *Cambridge Law Journal* 86; see also Sales, 'A Comparison' (2009) 125 *Law Quarterly Review* 598.

40 See Sales, 'A Comparison' (2009) 125 *Law Quarterly Review* 598.

41 For further discussion of these points, see Sales, 'Rights and Fundamental Rights' [2016] *Cambridge Law Journal* 86 and P. Sales, 'Modern Statutory Interpretation' (2017) 38 *Statute Law Review* 125.

42 *R v Secretary of State for the Home Department, ex p Simms* [2000] 2 AC 115, 131.

By contrast with the operation of the principle of legality at the level of interpretation of the statutory text, where a statutory power conferring a discretion on a public authority cannot be 'read down' under that principle of construction, an area of discretion is *ex hypothesi* left intact. The focus shifts from a constrained reading of the intention of Parliament as expressed in the text of the statute to an acceptance that Parliament intended to confer a discretion on the public authority for it to choose how to act. Even if in some circumstances the width of the discretion is reduced to some extent by reference to the same or similar constitutional rights or principles, it still exists in a substantive sense, because Parliament intends that it should. The question for the court when the principle of legality is invoked is not whether the *exercise* of a particular statutory power was lawful in a given case (the question to which the rationality test is directed), but rather whether the *scope* of the power itself is limited by the presumption that fundamental common law rights and principles cannot be overridden by general or ambiguous words. That is why it was stated in the *Spitalfields* case that the principle of legality involves a form of interpretive surgery in relation to the text of the statute, where that is necessary to reflect Parliament's intention as properly understood.[43]

Further, the doctrine of anxious (or heightened) scrutiny is capable of coming into play in relation to practically any statutory discretionary power, to introduce some constraint on the exercise of that discretion. It is also capable of coming into play in relation to the exercise of any prerogative or common law powers available for exercise by the executive according to their discretion,[44] so it is not necessarily tied to any statute. There is thus no necessary or precise correlation between the range of powers which exist for the executive and the circumstances in which heightened scrutiny may be required in the exercise of such discretion. Heightened scrutiny is required in any area where, because of the impact

43 *R (Spitalfields Historic Building Trust) v London Borough of Tower Hamlets* [2025] UKSC 11, para 72.

44 See P. Sales, 'Crown Powers, the Royal Prerogative and Fundamental Rights', ch 14 in H. Wilberg and M. Elliott, *The Scope and Intensity of Substantive Review: Traversing Taggart's Rainbow* (2015).

of a decision on a constitutional right or principle or especially important interests recognised by the law, the court finds that rationality requires a high level of confidence that the decision is indeed justified, which may limit the range of rational decisions available and may impose particular demands regarding the quality of reasoning or evidence relied upon. The same point can be made about the other end of the spectrum of variable intensity of rationality review, where light touch review is similarly justified as the appropriate standard according to identifiable constitutional factors, as explained above.

There are other important differences between the principle of legality and the doctrine of heightened scrutiny. First, the principle of legality is a form of constraint on what Parliament can do. It operates as a type of manner and form constraint: if Parliament wishes to legislate contrary to a constitutional right or principle, it must do so in clear terms.[45] By contrast, the doctrine of heightened scrutiny is a constraint on what the executive (or other public authorities) can do. A basic application of principles of the separation of powers under the UK's constitution suggests that the latter will be easier to justify normatively than the former. It is a strong thing for the courts to seek to impose interpretations of legislation which constrain the way in which parliamentary sovereignty is exercised, which is the powerful rule underlying the entire constitution. But imposing standards of behaviour on the executive in the name of the rule of law is a normal and justified function of the courts in administrative law. It is not at all the same for a court to introduce constraints upon valid parliamentary action. That normative difference indicates that there should be a significant normative gap between the principle of legality and the doctrine of heightened review and their effects. Under rationality review, it is the public authority's reasons for acting which are scrutinised. Under the principle of legality, it is Parliament's reasons for acting (i.e. for legislating in the terms of the statute in question) which are in issue. A court does not have authority to disqualify Parliament's

45 See chapter 3.

reasons; it only has authority to interpret what it has said, including by taking account of background assumptions it has made.

Secondly, the principle of legality has to take account of the way in which Parliament has exercised its authority by legislating. The typical form of legislation is to enact bright-line rules, unless Parliament expressly specifies otherwise and qualifies a rule by open-textured language, for example so as deliberately to impose a standard, such as reasonableness, rather than create a bright-line rule.[46] Where Parliament enacts a standard to be applied, rather than a rule, it necessarily confers a degree of discretionary authority on a court which is asked to make an evaluative judgment to apply that standard; or confers a discretion on an identified decision-maker who has to apply that standard, such as a minister. But where Parliament enacts a rule to be applied, there is no discretion. The mode of legislation is important, because it is particularly by enacting bright-line rules that Parliament exercises its authority in a way which directly secures outcomes which it intends to achieve, with no mediation according to the judgment of a court or an official.[47] Any modification of the interpretation of a statutory provision which a court can plausibly achieve by application of the principle of legality, having regard to the key points outlined above, will tend therefore to be relatively bright-line in effect, to avoid the impression that the court is just making something up.[48] It is not often plausible to take a bright-line statutory provision and then construe it as only applying if the relevant party (say, the executive)

46 On the difference between standards and rules, see F. Schauer, *Playing by the Rules: A Philosophical Examination of Rule-Based Decision-Making in Law and Life* (1991), chs 5–8; C. Sunstein, *Legal Reasoning and Political Conflict* (1996), chs 4–7; K. Sullivan, 'Foreword: The Justices of Rules and Standards' (1992) 106 *Harvard Law Review* 24; J. Waldron, *Thoughtfulness and the Rule of Law* (2023), 127 ('a standard is a norm that requires some evaluative judgment of the person who applies it, whereas a rule is a norm presented as the end product of evaluative judgments already made by the lawmaker').

47 Cf A. Scalia, 'The Rule of Law as a Law of Rules' (1989) 56 *University of Chicago Law Review* 1175: Scalia argues for the US Supreme Court to lay down bright-line rules in doctrine, rather than standards which operate on an 'all things considered' basis, as the best way to transmit the decision-making authority of the Supreme Court throughout the legal system.

48 See P. Sales, 'Legislative Intention, Interpretation and the Principle of Legality' (2019) 40 *Statute Law Review* 53.

can justify its application. Either it applies or, because of the operation of the principle of legality to exclude it from application in relation to a constitutional right or principle, it does not.

A clear, justified trigger point for the application of the principle of legality is required in order to be sure that its application corresponds with (and can be demonstrated by the court to correspond with) the intention of Parliament and does not involve the courts in improperly usurping a legislative power. The trigger point is an identified constitutional right or principle which it is presumed that Parliament did not intend to displace when it legislated. The operation of the principle of legality should reflect the strong normative imperative to read a statutory provision in a particular way, which is ordinarily to disapply general words where a constitutional right or principle applies, rather than to change them into a rule which is not bright-line in form.[49] Unspoken assumptions as to the meaning intended by Parliament do not plausibly take the form that words to the effect that 'you may do this' or 'you may not do that' are to be read as if they said 'you may do this only if so-and-so condition of justification is satisfied' or 'you may not do that unless so-and-so condition of justification is satisfied'. Accordingly, on this view, the principle of legality does not operate along a spectrum in the same way as the rationality standard, which has a graduated force of application matched by a graduated range of effect along a 'sliding scale of review'.

In both cases, however, it is the courts which are called upon to identify the underlying constitutional rights or principles which have sufficient normative force to qualify the meaning to be given to a statute (under the principle of legality) or to qualify the application of the rationality standard. Although the courts can only do this if the evidence from constitutional practice and common understandings warrants it (so that it is clearly not a legislative power), nonetheless it does mean that the courts

49 This limitation is inherent in the idea that a particular constitutional right or principle should be of such salience as to be obvious to Parliament when it legislates: see P. Sales, 'A Comparison', 605–606; P. Sales, 'Legislative Intention', 62. Also see Sales, 'Crown Powers, the Royal Prerogative and Fundamental Rights', 385–386, and J. Varuhas, 'The Principle of Legality' [2020] *Cambridge Law Journal* 578.

have a degree of agency in making the relevant evaluation of evidence and in identifying norms of constitutional law. The agency is increased by the demanding nature of the evaluative judgment required in the context of an unwritten constitution where political practice changes a lot, meaning that it can be difficult to distinguish normative statements from simple descriptions of what has happened at a particular time.[50] The need for courts to be able to justify such qualifications of legislative meaning or of the application of the rationality standard in this way means that the contours of the factors which have these normative effects are liable to be broadly similar.

The flexible nature of the concept of rationality in UK public law is well recognised, but doubts are sometimes expressed about the lack of clarity this involves[51] and about how it is possible for there to be a spectrum of different levels of rationality reflecting different intensities of judicial scrutiny. This seems to be in tension with what appears on its face to be a standard expressed as a general and simple requirement.[52]

The answer to the conundrum of a flexible rationality standard lies in the density, or otherwise, of background constitutional understandings common to the important actors in the UK polity (legislature, executive and courts) which form the context in which the administrative decision in question falls to be considered. It is not sufficient that the courts by themselves would seek to impose restrictions on the usual operation of the rationality standard, because that would undermine the intended operation of discretions according to Parliament's will (in the case of statutory powers) or according to the ambit of judgment allowed to the

50 Features which led J.A.G. Griffith to declare that the constitution simply is 'no more and no less than what happens': 'The Political Constitution' (1979) 42 *Modern Law Review* 1.

51 See, e.g., *R (Youssef) v Secretary of State for Foreign and Commonwealth Affairs* [20126] UKSC 3; [2016] AC 1457, para 55 (Lord Carnwath); *R (SAG) v Governing Body of Winchmore School* [2025] EWCA Civ 1335, para 126 (Elisabeth Laing LJ).

52 Which is how 'rationality' was introduced into the legal lexicon by Lord Diplock as a simplifying and standard concept: *Council of Civil Service Unions v Minister for the Civil Service* [1985] AC 374, 410–411.

executive by the common law (in the case of prerogative and common law powers). Where it is the exercise of a statutory power which is in issue, the primary source of the relevant background understandings will be the statutory scheme in which that power is embedded. However, even in that situation, there will be scope for argument by reference to other background understandings, not set out or directly reflected in the statute itself, but nonetheless capable of informing the rationality context in respect of an exercise of that power.

A rationality approach based on referring to the density of common background understandings with normative effect offers the advantages that, first, it allows the courts to spell out and articulate the underlying factors which drive the ebb and flow of intensity of review under the rationality heading, thereby promoting greater transparency and predictability of response; and, secondly, it allows scope for integrating in a more coherent and satisfactory way the judicial review standards to be applied in highly varied statutory contexts and also in relation to the Crown's prerogative and common law powers. There should be a common focus on identifying the criteria according to which the rationality of a measure may be assessed.

For heightened rationality review, although the contest is one between the court's assessment and that of the executive (rather than a contest with Parliament's apparent intention on an ordinary language reading of the statutory text, as is the case in relation to the principle of legality), the executive is still the primary decision-maker as authorised by Parliament. Also, it is often the case that an executive decision-maker, such as a minister, has a degree of democratic authority stemming from their accountability to Parliament and the electorate which is greater than the court's. Therefore the court has to be able to justify on objective grounds its intervention to strike down their action as irrational and unlawful. To do that, where heightened scrutiny is applied, the court has to be able to point to a clearly identifiable underlying constitutional right or principle or other powerful interest recognised by the law which is being infringed by the executive action in question, in order to explain why it is normatively acceptable to apply something other than the standard rationality approach. The standard rationality approach is itself an expression of the ambit of the discretion which, on the courts' established interpretation, Parliament intended should be conferred on the decision-maker, other things being equal. It operates as a well-established default rule which Parliament understands, and Parliament legislates in the light of it and implicitly endorses it.[53] To justify a departure from the regular application of that standard according to its usual *Wednesbury* formulation,[54] a normative justification has to be identified according to objective criteria. That is so whether the effect is to expand the degree of discretion inherent in the rationality standard, where light touch rationality review is applied, or to narrow it on a heightened scrutiny basis. This means there needs to be a set of reasonably determinate criteria in this area, as in relation to the principle of legality, to justify the departure from the standard approach. For heightened scrutiny, the normative impulse to justify the departure does not need to be so strong as under the principle of legality, because the normative effect is less powerful (since the meaning of the statutory rule is not being changed), but it still has to have force beyond an identifiable threshold to justify departure from the ordinary rationality standard.[55]

Strictly, in the case of rationality review, it might be better to speak of recognition of the contours of constitutional *values*, rather than rights, to convey the idea that in general terms they are defeasible in the sense that the decision-maker retains a discretion (albeit one which is more constrained than in other circumstances) to put other factors into the balance against them. This captures the fact that by this stage of the

53 See Sales, 'Rationality, Proportionality and the Development of the Law' (2013) 129 *Law Quarterly Review* 223; and the discussion of the intersection between legislative practice and interpretive practice in chapter 3.

54 *Associated Provincial Picture Houses Ltd v Wednesbury Corporation* [1948] 1 KB 223; *Council of Civil Service Unions v Minister for the Civil Service* [1985] AC 374, 410–411.

55 A good example of a judgment in which specific factors bearing on the intensity of review required are identified and weighed against each other in order to determine the appropriate degree of scrutiny is *R (KP) v Secretary of State for Foreign, Commonwealth and Development Affairs* [2025] EWHC 370 (Admin) (Chamberlain J).

analysis one has excluded the possibility that the text of the statute itself has to be read down by reference to the principle of legality, because the normative force of the constitutional value is not so strong as to constitute something amounting to a constitutional right or principle with power to affect the meaning of the statute (or because Parliament has deliberately legislated to override such a right or principle in order to confer a discretion on the decision-maker).

Nonetheless, the contours for application of heightened scrutiny under the rationality standard will follow a line which is similar to the line traced by the contours for application of the principle of legality, since the constitutional values in question will broadly reflect the same factors which, in the context of the principle of legality, give rise to relevant constitutional rights and principles as justifications for departing from the natural meaning of the statutory text. But, for the reasons explained above, they do so with a significant gap between the two lines, which represents the zone of discretion which Parliament intends the decision-maker to have in the former case.

There is a range of sources which inform judicial and public opinion and which together are capable of generating background understandings which may come to be widely shared so as to have strong normative force within what Jack Balkin calls a 'spectrum of plausibility' about constitutional legal claims.[56] 'Reasonableness is not a single set of correct views; rather it is a distribution of possible positions about which reasonable people might differ, bounded by other views that are off-the-wall. The boundaries of the reasonable and the unreasonable, which people use to judge legitimacy, are produced in social life, including through politics'.[57] However, if the courts wish to use these understandings to inform the principle of legality or rationality review, there is an onus on them to spell out what they are and the evidence for them.

56 J. Balkin, *Constitutional Redemption: Political Faith in an Unjust World* (2011), 180.
57 Ibid, 61.

The Courts' Role to Interpret the Constitution and Identify the Values Inherent in It

Fundamental principles and rights are treated as embedded in the constitution. These are what Maitland called points of high principle.[58] By virtue of their embedded nature, they form part of the presumptive constitutional order which Parliament is taken to respect, subject to its ability to override them by use of very clear language in a statute. Under the rationality standard, they form part of the presumptive constitutional order which the executive is obliged to take into account when deciding how to act.

The courts' role is to identify what principles and rights exist, the degree to which they are fundamental, and how in practical terms they are to be reconciled with the democratic principle as it applies both at the legislative level and at the level of executive action. Each level of this analysis involves the form of agency on the part of the courts which I have described.

The courts move beyond a 'faithful agent' model of their role,[59] if that is to be taken (implausibly) to require them simply to apply legislation construed purely in terms of linguistic meaning. The function of identifying constitutional values, rights and principles derived from disparate materials is itself an activity involving a form of agency. The courts have to decide if additional normative content has to be injected into the statute, to identify the true meaning which Parliament intended, or into any applicable rule of common law. The process is one of recognition and deduction from evidence, rather than invention. Still, this means that courts are partners in the promotion of the constitutional order, not purely passive agents.

The role of the courts has fluctuated over time in response to shifts in the nature of the state and corresponding shifts in the balance between

58 See the discussion in F.W. Maitland, *The Constitutional History of England* (1908), 526–539, 'The Definition of Constitutional Law'.

59 See K. Greenawalt, *Statutory and Common Law Interpretation* (2013), 8.

Dicey's three pillars of the constitution: sovereignty of Parliament, rule of law and convention.

I will highlight seven developments and then consider the two *Miller* cases. The underlying theme is how the courts have reacted to the expansion of the role of the state and of the power of the executive, combined with a sense that political controls via convention and political morality have been becoming attenuated and inadequate for the protection of important rights.

In the *Fire Brigades Union* case in 1995,[60] Lord Mustill noted these trends:

> It is a feature of the peculiarly British conception of the separation of powers that Parliament, the executive and the courts have each their distinct and largely exclusive domain. Parliament has a legally unchallengeable right to make whatever laws it thinks right. The executive carries on the administration of the country in accordance with the powers conferred on it by law. The courts interpret the laws, and see that they are obeyed. This requires the courts on occasion to step into the territory which belongs to the executive, to verify not only that the powers asserted accord with the substantive law created by Parliament but also that the manner in which they are exercised conforms with the standards of fairness which Parliament must have intended. Concurrently with this judicial function Parliament has its own special means of ensuring that the executive, in the exercise of delegated functions, performs in a way which Parliament finds appropriate. Ideally, it is these latter methods which should be used to check executive errors and excesses; for it is the task of Parliament and the executive in tandem, not of the courts, to govern the country. In recent years, however, the employment in practice of these specifically Parliamentary remedies has on occasion been perceived as falling short, and sometimes well short, of what was needed to bring the performance of the executive into line with the law, and with the minimum standards of fairness implicit in every Parliamentary delegation of a decision-making function. To avoid a vacuum in which the citizen would be left without protection against a misuse of executive powers the courts have had no option but to occupy the dead ground in a manner, and in areas of public life, which could not have been foreseen 30 years ago. For myself, I am quite

60 *R v Secretary of State for the Home Department, ex p. Fire Brigades Union* [1995] 2 AC 513.

> satisfied that this unprecedented judicial role has been greatly to the public benefit. Nevertheless, it has its risks, of which the courts are well aware. As the judges themselves constantly remark, it is not they who are appointed to administer the country.[61]

As explained there, changes in political controls and their effectiveness may have implications for the development of administrative law. The constitutional agency of the courts emerges from the role they have to monitor the changes occurring and to assess their significance, and in deciding at what point they give rise to legal effects. Lord Mustill emphasised the importance of maintaining an appropriate balance between the roles of Parliament, the executive and the courts against this background of change: 'Absent a written constitution much sensitivity is required of the parliamentarian, administrator and judge if the delicate balance of the unwritten rules evolved (I believe successfully) in recent years' is to be maintained.[62] Sensitivity to the workings of the political part of the constitution is required on all sides. If appropriate sensitivity is not displayed by parliamentarians and the executive, then in line with this legal and constitutional tradition that may require the courts to develop the law. This is a long-established pattern, as is illustrated by the following account of the development of administrative law.

Seven Stages in the Development of Administrative Law

First, by the early twentieth century even Dicey was prepared to admit the need for the development of a new administrative law to control executive action, something which had been notably absent from his account in *The Law of the Constitution*. In 1915 he wrote about how administrative law was developing, noting the application of new standards of administrative fairness to be applied by the courts, against a background

61 Ibid, 567.
62 Ibid, 567.

where ministerial responsibility subject to political scrutiny was not perceived to be an adequate safeguard.[63]

Second, there was the major revival and development of judicial review doctrine in the 1960s, exemplified by the trilogy of cases of *Ridge v Baldwin* (emphasis given to the obligation of fairness in the exercise of executive power),[64] *Padfield* (emphasis given to the obligation to use statutory powers for proper purposes)[65] and *Anisminic* (interpretation of statute in the light of the principle of access to justice).[66] These are regarded as landmark decisions because they signalled a significant shift in the way in which courts would approach the interpretation of powers in statute. As Lord Hodge has said, 'The development of administrative law in the second half of the twentieth century has indeed been a major legal development . . . as the incremental application and development of pre-existing principles in changed circumstances and in response to developing social needs.'[67] The changing social need to which legal doctrine responded was the greatly increased role of government and other executive bodies in the lives of citizens in the course of the twentieth century. Lord Hodge also suggests that changing social attitudes played a part: a decline in respect for and deference to established public institutions, and the rise of a more questioning attitude in society and a greater awareness of (or tendency to think in terms of) individual rights. As Martin Loughlin points out, the 'positivization of the basic rights of citizens has the potential to reconfigure the architecture of public law'.[68] A coherent approach to administrative law was developed

63 A.V. Dicey, "The Development of Administrative Law in England" (1915) 72 *Law Quarterly Review* 148.

64 [1964] AC 40. See S. Juss and M. Sunkin (eds), *Landmark Cases in Public Law* (2017), ch 2.

65 *Padfield v Minister of Agriculture, Fisheries and Food* [1968] AC 997. See Juss and Sunkin, *Landmark Cases*, ch 3.

66 *Anisminic Ltd v Foreign Compensation Commission* [1969] 2 AC 147. See Juss and Sunkin, *Landmark Cases*, ch 4.

67 Lord Hodge, "The Scope of Judicial Law-Making in Constitutional Law and Public Law" (2021) 26 *Judicial Review* 146, 148. See also Lord Diplock's description of the transformation of administrative law from about the 1950s: *Council of Civil Service Unions v Minister for the Civil Service* [1985] AC 374, 407–408.

68 M. Loughlin, *The Idea of Public Law* (2003), 114.

to reflect standards of good administration in the interest of citizens, as they came to be recognised by the courts. The historical context for this is well described by Joseph Jacob in *The Republican Crown*,[69] who recounts the public disquiet about the Crichel Down affair in 1954, involving high-handed treatment of landowners by civil servants, leading to the Franks Committee inquiry into administrative tribunals and inquiries of 1955–57.

Third, in the 1970s there was renewed concern about the effectiveness of control of executive power through norms of political morality. Nevil Johnson, in his 1977 book *In Search of the Constitution*,[70] identified the erosion of nineteenth-century style political morality under the pressures of modern politics and modern government and made the case that the rights of the individual should be restated and safeguarded, 'both those which are intended to protect him against the abuse of authority and those which establish his status as a citizen and from which his political obligations stem'.[71] He argued that this would restore authority to the UK's pattern of representative government whilst at the same time maintaining its respect for liberty under the law.

There was then a long period of single-party rule by the Conservatives from 1979. The domination of Parliament by one party in this way served again to call in question the effectiveness of political controls in relation to executive power. Senior judges like Lord Scarman and Lord Bingham called for greater legal controls and the incorporation of the European Convention on Human Rights into domestic law. In the 1980s the concept of 'anxious scrutiny' review was identified.[72] In the 1990s, in cases such as *Pierson*, the principle of legality was identified and given renewed force and prominence.[73] In this way the courts gave legal effect to a range

69 J. Jacob, *The Republican Crown: Lawyers and the Making of the State in Twentieth Century Britain* (1996), ch 5.
70 N. Johnson, *In Search of the Constitution* (1977).
71 Ibid, 197.
72 *R v Secretary of State for the Home Department, ex p Bugdaycay* [1987] AC 514.
73 See e.g. *R v Secretary of State for the Home Department, ex p Pierson* [1998] AC 539; *R v Secretary of State for the Home Department, ex p Simms* [2000] 2 AC 115, 131–132. For discussion see P. Sales, 'Rights and Fundamental Rights in English Law' [2006]

of individual rights identified by them with increasing specificity. In broad terms, this was justified by the courts on the basis that Parliament is taken to legislate for a liberal democracy in a constitutional state which observes the rule of law.[74] However, if such broad concepts are regarded as capable of injecting determinate content into a statutory rule, the scope for the law to be affected by changes in the understanding of these concepts across time, as identified by the courts, is clear.

Fourth, in 1998 the new Labour government passed the Human Rights Act 1998 to enhance legal enforcement of fundamental rights. Labour did this having had the experience of being out of power for some 18 years, which made it very conscious of the weakness of political controls in relation to executive power. In a work of 2004, Nevil Johnson argued, 'in recent times deference has largely collapsed and the very notion of elite rule is widely rejected. It follows that there are few social and moral resources available in society to impede the steady withering away of the customary practices by which the constitution itself has been extensively defined. We have, therefore, to face the fact that a customary constitution might in some circumstances require resort to an injection of the kind of explicit principles thought to be characteristic of codified constitutions if it is to survive'.[75] This perspective supports the general contribution of the Human Rights Act 1998 to the current constitutional settlement.[76]

Fifth, from the 1960s onwards there was a gradual extension of judicial review of the exercise of prerogative and common law powers of the Crown. This has followed an arc from *ex p Lain*,[77] through recognition in the *GCHQ* case[78] of the possibility of judicial control on the basis of

Cambridge Law Journal 86; Sales, 'A Comparison'; J. Varuhas, 'The Principle of Legality' [2020] *Cambridge Law Journal* 578.

74 *R (Anufrijeva) v Secretary of State for the Home Department* [2004] 1 AC 604, paras 28–31 (Lord Steyn).

75 N. Johnson, *Reshaping the British Constitution* (2004), 19–20.

76 See also S. Wallace, 'The Human Rights Act Under Siege: the Vulnerability of Fundamental Rights Protection under the UK Constitution' [2025] *Public Law* 648.

77 *R v Criminal Injuries Compensation Board, ex p Lain* [1967] 2 QB 864.

78 *Council of Civil Service Unions v Minister for the Civil Service* [1985] AC 374.

underlying principles (which one could describe as fundamental or constitutional), to quashing of the prorogation of Parliament in the second *Miller* case.[79] The result in the latter case was justified explicitly in terms of the requirements of principles fundamental to a polity having the character of a parliamentary democracy, namely to ensure that Parliament should be able to carry out its constitutional functions as legislature and as the body responsible for supervision of the executive.[80]

Sixth, the doctrine of legitimate expectations also developed in the late twentieth century as the courts gave legal protection to procedural and substantive legitimate expectations based on policies or assurances given by public authorities as to how they would exercise discretionary powers. The underlying justification for this development was increasingly put in terms of constitutional principle. At first, emphasis was given to the abuse of power which was said would occur if there was a change of policy by a public authority in circumstances where a person had relied upon an official statement of the policy to their detriment, but this had to be balanced against the constitutional responsibilities of the authority in question.[81] Later, a distinct justification was given based on a constitutional principle of good administration.[82] In *Lumba*, Lord Dyson said, 'The individual has a basic public law right to have his or her case considered under whatever policy the executive sees fit to adopt provided that the adopted policy is a lawful exercise of the discretion conferred by the statute';[83] a policy has to be followed unless there are good reasons for departing from it.[84] This approach was endorsed by the Supreme Court in *Mandalia*.[85] The entitlement of an individual to have a policy

79 *R (Miller) v Prime Minister* [2019] UKSC 41, [2020] AC 373 ('*Miller II*').
80 Ibid, paras 49–50.
81 See e.g. *R (Begbie) v Department of Education* [2000] 1 WLR 1115.
82 See *R (Nadarajah) v Secretary of State for the Home Department* [2005] EWCA 1363, para 68 (Laws LJ: an individual's right to have their case determined in accordance with policy is 'a requirement of good administration, by which public bodies ought to deal straightforwardly and consistently with the public').
83 *R (Lumba) v Secretary of State for the Home Department (JUSTICE intervening)* [2011] UKSC 12; [2012] 1 AC 245, para 35.
84 Ibid, para 26.
85 *Mandalia v Secretary of State for the Home Department* [2015] UKSC 59; [2015] 1 WLR 4546.

applied in their case (absent a sufficiently strong countervailing reason[86]) as a matter of good administration was taken to exist even where they were unaware of it at the time, so that no question of detrimental reliance could arise. Instead, the basic principle is in effect one of equality of treatment and protection against capricious and unjustified differentiation between persons falling within the scope of the policy. The result is that legal force is given to the internal controls exercised by the executive over itself, as described in chapter 2. In substance, the courts have recognised the constitutional importance of this form of control over executive power and have articulated the legal principles applicable in this new area of the law.

They have done so in a way which has been highly sensitive to constitutional considerations. A statement of policy by the government is not binding law, so in their articulation of the legitimate expectations doctrine the courts have been careful to ensure that there remains scope for the executive to depart from a policy if there is a sufficient justification by reference to the public interest to do so.

The courts have also articulated different standards for enforcement of policy assurances depending on whether they give rise to a procedural legitimate expectation (i.e. an expectation as to how a public authority will give consideration to the exercise of a discretionary power, for instance by promising to invite representations or to conduct a consultation) or a substantive legitimate expectation (i.e. an expectation regarding the substantive decision which will be made in the exercise of such a power, rather than as to the process by which that decision will be arrived at).[87] The courts will more readily treat the public authority as bound by a procedural legitimate expectation than by a substantive legitimate expectation. Identifying and enforcing a substantive legitimate expectation

86 Probably to be judged according to a test of whether the departure is proportionate in light of the countervailing public interest being pursued: *Nadarajah* [2005] EWCA Civ 1368, para 68; see J. Moffett et al., *Judicial Review: Principles and Procedure*, 2nd ed (2026), para 20.76.

87 See generally J. Moffett et al., *Judicial Review: Principles and Procedure*, 2nd ed (2026), ch 20; and see the discussion in P. Sales and K. Steyn, 'Legitimate Expectations in English Public Law: An Analysis' [2004] *Public Law* 564.

against an unwilling public authority should be exceptional because, in effect, it involves the court stepping in as decision-maker to dictate a particular result in a field which is covered by discretion conferred by law on the public authority, and in circumstances where the public authority on further reflection (after initially giving the assurance) may think that the best solution is to depart from it. It is to be expected that there would need to be particularly strong reasons to justify this. By contrast, where all that is sought to be upheld is a legitimate expectation as to the procedure to be followed before a substantive decision is made, there is much less intrusion into the sphere of substantive judgment for which the public authority has been designated as decision-maker. In addition, the court is then much closer to fulfilling its ordinary constitutional role to ensure that decisions are taken fairly, where it is the judge of fairness. If the public authority has itself stated that, for example, it will consult before deciding, then it is relatively straightforward for the court to say that this can be regarded as fair and that it represents a reasonable (and not excessively burdensome) standard of procedural justice, since the public authority had itself selected it. Moreover, it can be said that there is particular value in holding a public authority to its promise regarding such a procedure (which does not intrude substantially on its ultimate substantive decision) in order to foster public confidence in the administration, unless some especially good overriding reason can be shown to depart from it.

Also, mindful of the tension between enforcing an assurance which has been given and the impact of that on the usual requirements regarding the use of limited resources in the overall public interest, the courts sometimes seek to give a substantive legitimate expectation only a procedural effect. Where there has been a promise that a substantive benefit will be conferred, the legitimate expectation may be satisfied if the authority is required to consider whether to honour it, but is allowed to weigh it against other public interest factors.[88]

88 See e.g. *R (Bibi) v Newham BC* [2002] 1 WLR 237.

Seventh, the courts have increasingly analysed the balance to be struck between the role of the executive, Parliament and themselves in terms of the separation of powers. The courts have had to explain, carve out and delimit their role versus that of other agencies of the state. Separation of powers tends to be the framework in which they seek to do this. Separation of powers has gone up the legal agenda and has also become more finely tuned over the last 60 years or so. This is partly a result of the widening application of a 'principle of functional specialisation and responsibility' in the public sector and the 'ever-greater functional differentiation' of the concept of the Crown, standing for the executive.[89] A conception of specialised zones of policy-making by different agencies of the state has developed, and the courts have had to define where the boundaries are and then police them. This means the courts have had to address the boundary between law and politics, but also that between courts (using legal expertise) and specialist policy-makers (using other forms of expertise[90]). On both boundaries, the Diceyan concept of the rule of law as one set of rules for all has come under pressure, to be replaced by the concept of the rule of law as appropriate demarcation to secure what Sir Jack Beatson calls 'the balance of responsibilities'.[91] The connection between the rule of law and the separation of powers is thus made central. Contrary to the Diceyan conception of the rule of law, the courts have recognised a specialised domain of public law.[92]

89 Johnson, *Reshaping*, 63–64.

90 Such as expertise in foreign affairs (*R (Shvidler) v Secretary of State for Foreign, Commonwealth and Development Affairs* [2025] UKSC 30), in matters of national security (*R (Begum) v Special Immigration Appeals Commission* [2021] UKSC 7; [2021] AC 765), in planning policy (*R (Alconbury Developments Ltd) v Secretary of State for the Environment, Transport and the Regions* [2001] UKHL 23; [2003] 2 AC 295), or in economics and setting the frameworks for markets (e.g. *Evans v Barclays Bank Plc* [2025] UKSC 48).

91 Sir J. Beatson, *The Rule of Law and the Separation of Powers* (2021), 123.

92 See also Johnson, *Reshaping*, 149–153.

The Growing Importance of a Separation of Powers Doctrine Articulated by the Courts

The application of human rights under the Human Rights Act 1998 and the principle of legality, and the proportionality standard of review associated with those rights and with the doctrine of legitimate expectation arising from government statements of policy, have drawn courts more into the realm of specification of policy. This has meant that the courts have had to articulate with greater care and specificity the proper limits of their role as against other agencies. By doing this the courts seek to defend a zone of law distinct from politics and policy, which are recognised as properly being the subject of political contestation or specialist evaluation.[93] Witness the *Alconbury* case in relation to the implementation of planning policy,[94] for example, and the *SC* decision in relation to setting the parameters of entitlement for welfare benefits.[95] Section 3 of the Human Rights Act 1998 has given the courts an enhanced interpretive role which is quasi-legislative, so the courts have had to explain how far they can go in modifying the meaning of legislation so as not to undermine the essence of the legislature's role.[96]

Public law has increasingly come to be concerned with functional specialisation and the response of the courts to this in the light of underlying constitutional principles of the rule of law and democracy, for which parliamentary sovereignty stands as a cipher. Both have implications for the separation of powers, as a series of Supreme Court judgments illustrate. In *Majera*[97] the court emphasised the obligation of the executive to obey

93 E.g. by a designated agency, such as in *R v Monopolies and Mergers Commission, ex p South Yorkshire Transport Ltd* [1993] 1 WLR 23 (HL), discussed in Beatson, *The Rule of Law*, 129–130.

94 *R (Alconbury Developments Ltd) v Secretary of State for the Environment, Transport and the Regions* [2001] UKHL 23; [2003] 2 AC 295.

95 *R (SC) v Secretary of State for Work and Pensions* [2021] UKSC 26.

96 The leading case is *Ghaidan v Godin-Mendoza* [2004] UKHL 30; [2004] 2 AC 557.

97 *R (Majera) v Secretary of State for the Home Department* [2021] UKSC 46.

a court order. In *SC*[98] the court emphasised the width of the margin of appreciation for Parliament on matters of economic and social policy. In *Begum*,[99] following the *Rehman* decision,[100] the court emphasised the responsibility of the executive for judgments about national security, on grounds of democratic accountability and expertise. In *Privacy International*[101] the court divided where there was a collision between different aspects of these principles.

All these shifts in doctrine exemplify the exercise of constitutional agency by the courts. The aim has been to maintain an underlying constitutional balance between the roles of the executive, Parliament and the courts across time, under circumstances where the balance between the pillars of the constitution described by Dicey has come under pressure and has changed.

The requirement that the executive and legislature respect constitutional norms means that the constitution slows down the tempo of executive time and legislative time, and this is capable of having a calming effect on politics. This aids legitimacy as well and reinforces loser consent. It gives reassurance that minority views have been considered and not lost in the rush to get things done.

The liberal democratic system can only function effectively if respect for it and consequently for the laws it produces is maintained across time. As Hegel observed:

> How blind they are who may hope that institutions, constitutions, laws which no longer correspond to human manners, needs and opinions, from which the spirit has flown, can subsist any longer; or that forms in which intellect and feeling now take no interest are powerful enough to be any longer the bond of a nation![102]

98 *R (SC) v Secretary of State for Work and Pensions* [2021] UKSC 26.

99 *R (Begum) v Special Immigration Appeals Commission* [2021] UKSC 7; [2021] AC 765.

100 *Secretary of State for the Home Department v Rehman* [2001] UKHL 47; [2003] 1 AC 153.

101 *R (Privacy International) v Investigatory Powers Tribunal* [2019] UKSC 22; [2020] AC 491.

102 Z.A. Pełczyński (ed), *Hegel's Political Writings*, trans TM Knox (1964), 243–244.

Miller I and *Miller II*

Against this background I turn to examine the two *Miller* cases.

Miller I[103] concerned the giving of notice under article 50 of the Treaty on the European Union for the UK to leave the EU. In conceptual terms this is not a difficult case. It concerned the interpretation of a statute, the European Communities Act 1972. The question was, had Parliament left it open to the executive to neutralise the effect of that Act by unilateral withdrawal from the EU by giving notice of such withdrawal without parliamentary authorisation? Both the Divisional Court[104] and the Supreme Court held that it had not. One can debate the result, but the task to be carried out and the methodology to be applied were straightforward.

Miller II was more difficult.[105] It concerned the lawfulness of the prorogation of Parliament during the Brexit crisis concerning negotiation with the EU of the terms of the UK's withdrawal. The power of prorogation is a matter for the prerogative, not statute. So the courts had to address the issue in the context of the less developed law concerning the prerogative and the control of its exercise in modern times.

The case stands in the line of development of public law over the past 70 years which I have mapped out above. The argument for the government was that the exercise of this prerogative power was non-justiciable because of the political context and the availability of political control through standards of political morality and the theoretical power of MPs to vote down the government on a confidence motion. But these claims had to be assessed in the light of the erosion of customary standards of political behaviour over decades and a general loss of confidence in them. They also had to be assessed in terms of what was at stake and in terms of

103 *R (Miller) v Secretary of State for Exiting the European Union* [2017] UKSC 5 ('*Miller I*').

104 *R (Miller) v Secretary of State for Exiting the European Union* [2016] EWHC 2768 (Admin). I was a member of the Divisional Court which gave this judgment.

105 *R (Miller) v The Prime Minister* [2019] UKSC 41 ('*Miller II*'). I was a member of the 11 Justice constitution of the Supreme Court which delivered this judgment.

how directly implicated, and how at risk, were recognised fundamental features of the constitution, as regards parliamentary sovereignty and the role of Parliament in holding the government to account as a basic incident of responsible government.

The Supreme Court was acutely aware of the political context. It emphasised that the case was a one off. However, it had to confront a situation in which, in a particularly acute way, the erosion of the conventional part of the constitution meant it had to choose between finding that one had hit the bedrock of *law* in the constitutional order, which the court had a role to enforce, or finding that there was no effective control at all over such a momentous executive decision. The government conceded during the hearing that the involvement of the monarch did not constitute a significant control, because the Queen was constitutionally bound (and would in any event feel compelled in practice) to act on the advice of the Prime Minister, whose decision was under review.[106]

The Supreme Court quashed the advice and the decision which flowed from it, meaning that the purported prorogation was of no effect. The judgment was the product of the very unusual circumstances in which the case arose. It is not a harbinger of a general move to unjustified judicial activism in the extension of legal norms regarding control of the executive.

Four points should be emphasised. One is the extremity of the claim being presented by the government. The government made no attempt to justify the decision to prorogue by reference to some public policy objective. It did not present evidence to say that it had made a political judgment that it was necessary to suspend Parliament in order to improve its

106 In the past, in relation to colonial or Commonwealth affairs, the monarch, acting by his or her representative, the local Governor-General, has adopted a more substantive constitutional role: see A. Twomey, *The Veiled Sceptre: Reserve Powers of Heads of State in Westminster Systems* (2018). But the monarch's role in relation to political affairs in the UK itself has always been more circumscribed in particular ways, e.g. in relation to the withholding of Royal Assent for legislation: see A.V. Dicey, *Introduction to the Study of the Law of the Constitution*, 8th ed (1908), 110. It was not realistic to suppose that in the fraught political context of Brexit the Queen could have done other than act as a cipher and follow the advice of the Prime Minister in relation to the prorogation decision.

hand in the negotiations with the EU. That would have posed a difficult issue for the court, since it would then have had to weigh up the force of the aspects of the democratic principle and the principle of responsible government which would be infringed by suspension of Parliament at such a critical time in the life of the nation against other aspects of those principles which would have been in issue, involving the judgment of the elected government regarding the conduct of the UK's foreign affairs. I do not speculate how the court might have reacted to such a case. It was never made.

Instead, the government's argument was that the prorogation decision was of such political moment that it had to be regarded as non-justiciable so that it was outside the jurisdiction of the courts to pronounce upon its legality. This was an extreme claim regarding the boundaries between law and politics under the UK constitution. It mistook the undoubtedly strongly political nature of the constitution as meaning that there was no constitutional *law* to be applied at all regarding that decision. In my view, that was always an implausible claim. Under the UK's constitution there is a deep layer of political custom and practice before one comes to the level of law, but that does not mean that law is completely absent. The UK's constitution is founded on constitutional principles which have normative force, and there is in principle always a point at which the normative force of those principles might be capable of having effect as law which the court will apply, as distinct from being left as a matter of political convention.

Under the UK's unwritten constitution that point may sometimes be difficult to identify precisely, but if the courts have any responsibility at all under the constitution it is to identify what is or is not law, even where that is difficult to do. The fact that 11 Justices unanimously held that the prorogation decision violated applicable constitutional principles in a profound way is some evidence, at least, that in the circumstances of the case it was not ultimately difficult to identify that the point had been reached where those principles assumed the quality of law, and that in the absence of any justification that law had been violated.[107] Just how far

107 See *Miller II*, para 57: the Prime Minister's advice to the Queen had 'an extreme effect upon the fundamentals of our democracy', such that 'a reasonable justification' was required. None was given.

the government's position represented a departure from political norms is underlined by the fact that a former Prime Minister, Sir John Major,[108] intervened in the case to explain the conventional practice in relation to prorogation of Parliament—which is to allow a short period for the preparation of a statement of the government's legislative programme to be presented in the next Queen's (or King's) speech; to protest that there was no legitimate basis for the government's attempt to secure a five-week period of prorogation; and to support the claim that this was in violation of constitutional law.

The government's submission in *Miller II* meant that it was committed to a case that on the first day of a Parliament the government could require the monarch to prorogue it and keep it out of action indefinitely, involving an absolutely fundamental breach of the constitutional principles regarding the role of Parliament and how responsible government is supposed to work. The fact that the government adduced no evidence to justify what it had done served to emphasise the extremity of the claim. One assumes that no evidence was filed precisely in order to do that. The government wished to secure a ruling from the court that would absolve it from any legal constraints whatever as regards such a decision.

The second point is the time-critical nature of what was at stake. The UK was negotiating and seeking to finalise a new treaty with the EU which would have profound political, economic and constitutional implications for the UK. This was a matter which Parliament had actively been reviewing and in relation to which it was seeking to exercise a measure of control over what the government was doing. This would seem to be a matter in which the principles of parliamentary sovereignty and of the accountability of government to Parliament were engaged in a particularly direct and powerful way. Disablement of Parliament at such a juncture would have undermined them fatally.

Third, it was an unusual feature of the situation in Parliament that the ordinary processes of collective decision-making there had broken

108 Of the same political party (the Conservatives) as Boris Johnson.

down. The government could not command a majority in support of its policy. The political divisions around Brexit cut across the party system, so the usual party mechanisms to negotiate a way through to a parliamentary majority for a course of action were clearly not operating. The special statutory provisions in place under the Fixed-Terms Parliament Act 2011[109] cut across the usual position under the UK constitution that a Prime Minister is able to advise the monarch to dissolve Parliament, and this led to the atypical outcome that ordinary MPs were in control of that process. The importance and urgency of the negotiations with the EU meant that they were not willing to do that, which had the effect that the executive government was in a sense a prisoner of Parliament in a highly unusual way. But there were no settled procedures which enabled Parliament to arrive at a determinative decision. Every positive proposal to settle on a way forward with the EU was voted down by different combinations of MPs. Parliament was shown to be at once powerful and powerless. It was able to prevent its own dissolution, but not able to decide how to proceed. In these circumstances there could be no assurance that ordinary political procedures would allow for effective political controls to operate in relation to the Prime Minister's decision to suspend Parliament. Timothy Endicott writes that the inaction of MPs by not proceeding to pass a motion of no confidence in the government, which under the terms of the 2011 Act would have triggered a general election, is 'an indictment of the House of Commons'.[110] Maybe so, but the effect was to heighten the responsibility of the court to decide whether a point had been reached where fundamental constitutional principles came to the surface in the form of constitutional law.

In constitutional contexts in many jurisdictions it is a familiar pattern that where a legislature is not functioning as it should, the responsibility of the courts to play a more active role to secure the common good is increased and has an effect on their approach to the identification of relevant legal norms. Nick Barber observes that the failure of

109 Which was repealed in 2022.

110 T. Endicott, 'Making Constitutional Principles into Laws' (2020) 136 *Law Quarterly Review* 175, 176. Endicott is one of the critics of the judgment in *Miller II*.

one organ in the constitution can lead to a sort of 'constitutional inflation' in relation to the usual role of other organs; the most common example being that

> when the legislature is malfunctioning in some way—perhaps it lacks democratic legitimacy for some reason or it has become deadlocked and unable to legislate—this sometimes leads to the courts modifying their law-making role in response, becoming more willing to radically interpret existing legislation or make decisions that depart from existing law.[111]

Whether one describes it as 'constitutional inflation' or rational development of the law, this has been and continues to be the tradition in the development of administrative and constitutional law in the UK, as outlined above. The tradition has not created law which is frozen at any given point in time; on the contrary, it is a tradition precisely because it reacts to changing circumstances but in accordance with underlying and enduring principles.

Fourthly, the deep historical dimension in relation to *Miller II* is not always appreciated. Before the Glorious Revolution of 1688 laid the foundations for parliamentary sovereignty and responsible government, James II had used the power of prorogation to stop Parliament deliberating when he found that inconvenient.[112] The Glorious Revolution was aimed in part against preventing precisely this sort of abuse. After James II fled, a committee of the House of Commons drew up the Heads of Grievances for presentation to William of Orange. These were the basis for the Declaration of Rights, which became the Bill of Rights. The Heads of Grievances stated that Parliament 'ought to sit frequently' and that there should be 'no interruption of any session of Parliament, till the

111 N.W. Barber, *The Principles of Constitutionalism* (2018), 232–233. And see the discussion in P. Sales, 'Law, Democracy and the Absent Legislator', ch 10 in E. Fisher, J. King and A. Young (eds), *The Foundations and Future of Public Law* (2020).

112 T. Harris, *Revolution: The Great Crisis of the British Monarchy 1685–1720* (2006), 68–73, 96–100 (the first English Parliament of James II's reign convened on 19 May 1685, proved recalcitrant and was prorogued on 20 November 1685; James did not call another Parliament in England until the end of his reign in 1688); Maitland, *Constitutional History*, 296.

affairs that are necessary to be dispatched at that time are determined'.[113] Article 13 of the Bill of Rights stated that 'for the redress of all grievances and for the amending, strengthening and preserving of the Lawes, Parliaments ought to be held frequently'.[114] The basic principle remains the same in the twenty-first century, but the imperative to maintain parliamentary control over critical decisions affecting the future of the country has grown stronger with the increased importance of the democratic principle as a foundation of the constitution.

There has, of course, been a great deal of commentary about *Miller II*, some strongly supportive of the judgment and some strongly critical of it. In my opinion, an article by Erin Delaney presents a perceptive measured assessment from a comparative law perspective which comes close to the mark.[115] Delaney correctly emphasises the one-off nature of the judgment, which was on one view outside the bounds of British constitutional orthodoxy, but was nonetheless a legitimate reaction in law to government action which was itself profoundly outside the bounds of British constitutional orthodoxy and customary practice. Many constitutional courts find it appropriate to invoke, *in extremis*, legal principles arising from the basic structure of the constitutions in their jurisdiction, even though they are only implicit and are not expressly spelled out in terms of the relevant written constitutional instrument, in order to control executive action which puts that structure in jeopardy in a serious way. She refers to an article by Rosalind Dixon and David Landau which analyses the basic structure doctrine as it is invoked in such cases,[116] rooting the doctrine 'in a kind of democratic pragmatism'[117] and arguing that resort to the doctrine is justified when an attempt to amend the

113 Harris, *The Great Crisis*, 331–332.

114 Ibid, 345–346.

115 E. Delaney, 'The UK's Basic Structure Doctrine: *Miller II* and Judicial Power in Comparative Perspective' (2022) XII *Notre Dame Journal of International and Comparative Law* 22.

116 R. Dixon and D. Landau, 'Transnational Constitutionalism and a Limited Doctrine of Unconstitutional Constitutional Amendment' (2015) 13 *International Journal of Constitutional Law* 606.

117 Delaney, 'Basic Structure', 31.

constitution 'poses a real risk to democratic constitutionalism' itself.[118] Concerns about the legitimacy of courts intervening in such cases 'are mitigated in the face of measures which work "to cut off future exercises of democratic decision-making" or function "to allow leaders to increase their hold on power or to undermine institutions that were previously acting as a check"'.[119] Delaney analyses the context in which *Miller II* was decided and concludes that it was 'certainly plausible for a court to have concluded that responsible government was in some peril and that a five week prorogation in these circumstances was a step too far'.[120]

Miller II has its place in a strand of authority which exemplifies the working of the British constitution. There is a series of political principles which underpin the constitution and provide its basic orientation. Under circumstances of stress, when political conventions, custom and practice are eroded, these can come to the surface in legal form.

Other instances of this process in action are the account given by Lord Mustill in *Fire Brigades Union* of the development of legal principles of judicial review as a response to the erosion of political practices of control of the administration through Parliament;[121] the way in which the principle of the rule of law and access to the courts creates specifically legal effects through the principle of legality, or even (in the view of some judges) as a limit on the sovereignty of Parliament, as illustrated by *Privacy International*;[122] and this observation in *Moohan v Lord Advocate*,[123] a case concerning legislative regulation of the right to vote:

> While the common law cannot extend the franchise beyond that provided by parliamentary legislation, I do not exclude the possibility that in the very unlikely event that a parliamentary majority abusively sought to entrench its power by a curtailment of the franchise or similar device, the common law, informed by principles of democracy and the rule of law and international norms, would be able to declare such legislation unlawful.

118 Ibid., 32, quoting Dixon and Landau.
119 Ibid., 32, quoting Dixon and Landau.
120 Ibid., 32–38.
121 See pp. 98–99 above.
122 See p. 71 above.
123 [2014] UKSC 67; [2015] AC 901, at para 35 (Lord Hodge).

However, because the constitution has such a strong and deep political element, the circumstances in which this legal surfacing occurs are unusual and rare. Thus in *Moohan*, for example, the challenge to exclusion of certain persons from voting was disposed of by application of entirely conventional principles of statutory interpretation.

5

Conclusion

Robert Crowcroft argues that an important component of British national identity is constitutional, in that for many citizens Parliament represents 'the epicentre of the lawful social order'.[1] However, there is plenty of commentary to the effect that respect for politicians and for the political order has declined.

As mentioned in chapter 1, in order for the constitution to command public acceptance and underpin consent for the government's rule, there has to be a degree of emotional loyalty to it. In the eighteenth and nineteenth centuries there was a powerful narrative surrounding the British constitution as a constitution of freedom.[2] J.G.A. Pocock draws attention to the link between historiography and sovereignty. Definitions of historiography have a political dimension: 'They presuppose that one of the aims of the state is to exercise some control over its own history, defining its past and seeking to determine its future; that the liberal state associates individuals with it in this enterprise, that of seeking the freedom . . . to act as citizens in the determination of their own historicized identities; that political sovereignty was so far the state's means of prescribing its historic past and future that it was doubtful whether the

1 R. Crowcroft, 'Political Parties', ch 17 in P. Cane and H. Kumarasingham (eds), *The Cambridge Constitutional History of the United Kingdom*, vol I (2023), 453.

2 See the account in H. Kumarasingham, 'The Historical Constitution', ch 1 in P. Cane and H. Kumarasingham (eds), *The Cambridge Constitutional History of the United Kingdom*, vol I (2023).

Constitutional Agency. Philip Sales, Oxford University Press. © Philip Sales 2026.
DOI: 10.1093/oso/9780197928370.003.0005

individual could be accounted free . . . unless a citizen of an autonomous and sovereign political community'.[3]

Maurizio Viroli argues that a constitution should be sustained by a patriotic sense of the value it has demonstrated over time and the freedom it has sustained and still sustains for its citizens.[4] He writes: 'The language of patriotism has been used over the centuries to strengthen or invoke love of the political institutions and the way of life that sustain the common liberty of a people, that is love of the republic', emphasising that this is very different from the language of nationalism forged in late eighteenth-century Europe to defend or reinforce the cultural, linguistic and ethnic oneness and homogeneity of a people.[5] Although there is a limit to how far the courts can contribute to this form of constitutional patriotism informed by our history,[6] they do in fact do so by their day-to-day practice of giving effect to proper standards of governmental behaviour in accordance with constitutional values. They should be sure to remind the readers of their judgments that the UK constitution gives expression to an ethic of freedom of the individual and of the nation.

The motifs of the liberal democracy which is the UK are freedom, solidarity and hope. Freedom is the freedom of self-determination in its individual and collective aspects, both of which are important for the legitimacy of the regime. A sense of solidarity is necessary to constitute the *demos* and to allow for effective collective decision-making while at the same time promoting respect between citizens with conflicting views and ensuring that they are accorded political equality and protection.

3 J.G.A. Pocock, *The Discovery of Islands: Essays in British History* (2005), 279.

4 M. Viroli, *For Love of Country* (1995).

5 Ibid, 1.

6 Cf the concept of 'constitutional patriotism' proposed by Jurgen Habermas, which can seem too abstract and cerebral. As Viroli writes in *For Love of Country*, 173, 'If we rely only on universalist reasons, as Habermas does, without resorting to arguments that refer to a "common history and common origin", we cannot understand or encourage civic solidarity. A political culture sustained by motivations for the common good can exist only if rooted in national tradition and identity. The civic loyalty and solidarity that democracy needs to work does not simply stem from the universalistic principle of citizenship, but requires the identity with the concrete cultural and political community that we call "nation"'.

Hope, in the shape of the possibility of changing hostile political opinions and outcomes today to positive opinions and outcomes in the future, is necessary to bind citizens into the political regime.

The constitutional order has to give effect to these values and find ways of giving expression to them. In that way the constitution can be a focus for public loyalty and commitment.

There are two major arguments for framing the constitution of the UK by reference to the values of freedom under the law and responsible government in the way I have sought to do, including as they have developed to incorporate the principles of the rule of law and democracy. First, these fundamental features of the constitution have made a significant contribution to the survival of the British state and to its success over hundreds of years; and as Harshan Kumarasingham puts it, 'constitutional history exists to speak precedent unto power'.[7] Their value has been tested and vindicated through hard historical experience of crisis, threat and challenge to the British state over a very long period. They are principles which promote individual initiative and the contribution that can make to society, and political flexibility and adaptability in the face of problems and threats. They have allowed state power to be constructed for the benefit of citizens under conditions where it is regarded as legitimate. This is not something to be brushed aside lightly. It would be unwise to abandon them.

Secondly, they are values which, in the modern world, have an obvious attraction. Freedom under the law means that an individual has autonomy to choose how to live their own life. Responsible government and democracy are the bases for self-rule at a collective level, based on an ethic of equality. The UK's constitution seeks to give full weight, so far as possible, to each of these values and to provide a stable and coherent mechanism for accommodating tensions between them. It provides for a practical juxtaposition of a liberal tradition of individual rights and freedoms with a tradition of democratic self-government.[8]

7 Kumarasingham, 'The Historical Constitution', 3.

8 On the deep roots of these traditions in Western political discourse see e.g. C. Mouffe, *The Return of the Political* (1993), esp. chs 7–9; C. Mouffe, *The Democratic Paradox* (2000); and R. Geuss, *History and Illusion in Politics* (2001), esp. ch 3; Jurgen Habermas,

I do not seek to present an argument for an unthinking return to the triumphalist and complacent view of the British constitution which prevailed in the high Victorian age.[9] That was the product of the UK's economic and geopolitical success as the state which was the first to undergo and benefit from the Industrial Revolution. As other states have caught up with the UK and it has fallen back in terms of relative position, 'the authority of the British constitutional inheritance has waned'.[10]

But although relative economic decline may have removed grounds for complacency, what should remain is a real sense of the value of the UK's constitutional arrangements as a mechanism to integrate individual and collective freedom. They enable the inhabitants of the UK to sustain a common life with benefits for all, while holding back the forces of political entropy and decay.[11] It is by these means that the state can avoid being overwhelmed by an extreme friend/enemy distinction which Carl Schmitt placed at the heart of political life,[12] while allowing for a political culture of agonistic pluralism and contestation.[13]

The political orientation of the UK's constitution is a strength. It recognises and accepts 'the impossibility of a world without antagonism'[14] and seeks to provide a practical mechanism to maintain a pluralistic democratic order under those conditions, in which political opponents are identified and accepted as adversaries rather than rejected as enemies.[15] Citizens are held together by a sense of solidarity based on a

"Constitutional Democracy: A Paradoxical Union of Contradictory Principles?" (2001) 29 *Political Theory* 766 (trans. William Rehg).

9 Kumarasingham, 'The Historical Constitution', gives a good account of this.

10 As Martin Loughlin puts it in *Foundations of Public Law* (2010), 5.

11 See J. Dunn, *The Cunning of Unreason: Making Sense of Politics* (2000).

12 C. Schmitt, *The Concept of the Political*, trans. George Schwab ([1932] 1996).

13 Mouffe, *The Return of the Political* (1993); C. Mouffe, *Agonistics: Thinking the World Politically* (2013). See also E-W. Böckenförde, 'The Concept of the Political: A Key to Understanding Carl Schmitt's Constitutional Theory' in D. Dyzenhaus (ed), *Law as Politics: Carl Schmitt's Critique of Liberalism* (1998).

14 Cf Waldron's conception of 'the circumstances of politics': J. Waldron, *Law and Disagreement* (1999), 102 ('the felt need . . . for a common framework or decision or course of action on some matter, even in the face of disagreement about what that framework, decision or action should be').

15 Mouffe, *The Return of the Political*, 4. See also Mouffe, *Democratic Paradox*, 102 ('An adversary is an enemy, but a legitimate enemy, one with whom we have some common

shared history which enables 'the state as a political unity to relativize domestic antagonisms, tensions and conflicts so as to facilitate peaceful debates as well as solutions and ultimately decisions that are in accordance with procedural standards of argumentation and public discourse'.[16] The UK's constitution should be seen as one which allows for, indeed encourages, healthily robust political debate 'within the context of a specific political association defined by an idea of the common good . . . understood in strictly political terms [rather than substantive moral or religious terms], as the political common good of a liberal democratic regime'.[17]

This vision is capable of inspiring loyalty. If the principal task of a modern and democratic political philosophy is the articulation of individual liberty and political liberty,[18] the same task exists in a concrete and practical sense for constitutional law. As another commentator on Schmitt puts it, one lesson to be drawn from his work is that 'philosophical liberalism has to be given political and historical expression, rather than being presented as a moral philosophy. It will then be in a better position to cope with "contradiction, complexity, diversity, and the risks of freedom"'.[19]

Judith Shklar argued for what she called a 'liberalism of fear',[20] that is to say, a liberal regime with practical safeguards against cruelty and

ground because we have a shared adhesion to the ethico-political principles of liberal democracy').

16 Böckenförde, 'The Concept of the Political', 39.

17 Mouffe, *The Return of the Political*, 47.

18 Ibid, 57.

19 J-W. Müller, *A Dangerous Mind: Carl Schmitt in Post-War European Thought* (2003), 250 (quoting J. Sklar, *Ordinary Vices* (1984), 5). See also Dunn, *The Cunning of Unreason*, 363: 'Human beings have done many more fetching and elegant things than invent and routinize the modern democratic republic. But, in the face of their endlessly importunate, ludicrously indiscreet, inherently chaotic and always potentially murderous onrush of needs and longings, they have, even now, done very few things as solidly to their advantage . . . we do owe it our loyalty'.

20 J. Shklar, *Ordinary Vices* (1984), ch 6; J. Shklar, 'The Liberalism of Fear' in S. Hoffmann (ed). *Political Thought and Political Thinkers* (1998). For discussion of the idea of domination, and why freedom under the law is a safeguard against it, see Q. Skinner, 'States and the Freedom of Citizens', ch 1 in Q. Skinner and B. Strath, *States and Citizens: History, Theory, Prospects* (2003).

domination, which protects from predation by unconstrained governing elites[21] or by an irrational mob driven by emotion. Montesquieu was one of her heroes: 'The real point for Montesquieu . . . is not to paint the free citizen as a virtuous person, but to insist that without freedom everyone is intolerably paralyzed or demeaned . . . That is why there cannot be a price set on liberty'.[22] Montesquieu regarded England as unique, because it was 'the one nation in the world whose constitution has political liberty for its direct purpose'.[23] Bernard Williams argued for a similar political conception of liberalism, a 'liberalism of fear' founded on practical experience rather than political theory.[24] The liberalism of fear 'is bottom-up, not top-down', taking 'the condition of life without terror as its first requirement' and regarding 'the discovery of what rights people have as a political and historical one, not a philosophical one'.[25] This is an idea of legitimacy that provides public reasons to people of very different philosophical views to accept the exercise of power, not on the grounds of a moral conception of personhood or for abstract theoretical reasons, 'but instead on the grounds of historical experience'.[26] Paul Sagar supports Williams' political conception of liberalism and comments, 'if we want to know more about our political history and the best ways of preventing cruelty, progress is most likely to be made not by considering values and concepts in the abstract, but in examining what has been found to work in experience', so that a sound appreciation of what the liberalism of fear can achieve for us 'may turn out to lie more

21 To guard against them being 'transported by their passions into all the excesses of cruelty and ambition', as David Hume put it in *A Treatise of Human Nature* (1739), Book III, Part II, Section IX, and recognising that, in Lord Acton's adage, power tends to corrupt and absolute power corrupts absolutely.

22 Shklar, *Ordinary Vices*, 235.

23 Montesquieu, *The Spirit of the Laws* (1748), Book 11, chapter 5.

24 B. Williams, 'The Liberalism of Fear'. ch 5 in B. Williams, *In the Beginning was the Deed: Realism and Moralism in Political Argument* (2005).

25 Ibid, 61.

26 P. Sagar, 'From Scepticism to Liberalism? Bernard Williams, the Foundations of Liberalism and Political Realism' (2016) 64 *Political Studies* 368, 380, quoting F. Freyenhagen, 'Taking Reasonable Pluralism Seriously: An Internal Critique of Political Liberalism' (2011) 10 *Politics, Philosophy and Economics* 323, 336.

in the disciplines of jurisprudence, the history of political thought and constitutional analysis'.[27]

In this book I have sought to make the case that the UK constitution, seen as a developing enterprise through time based on certain fundamental principles, gives powerful political and historical expression to the values of individual and collective freedom. The book presents an argument for a form of constitutional patriotism grounded in a shared history.

The principles of individual freedom, the rule of law and collective self-government through democracy and the structures of responsible government are sufficiently substantive as to provide a basic orientation for constitutional debate and the development of constitutional law. They are reference points to which appeal may be made. At the same time, they are sufficiently abstract as to allow scope for flexibility in working through their detailed application under the pressures and in the ebb and flow of political life.

As Machiavelli emphasised, republics, like religions, have to change to sustain themselves against those pressures through time;[28] but to do this while remaining true to their political identity and the basic values which they reflect and exist to promote, they have to constantly have in mind and seek to hold faith with the basic principles which are the foundation for their constitution: 'In Order for a Religion or a Republic to Have a Long Life, It Is Often Necessary to Bring it Back to its Beginnings'.[29] Adrian Vermeule also employs an analogy between constitutional law and the development of religious doctrine which manages to preserve its fundamental identity across time whilst adapting in light of changes in

27 Sagar, ibid, 381. See also J. Waldron, *Political Political Theory* (2016), ch 1. Waldron supports Montesquieu's emphasis on forms, processes and structures of government, 'the deliberative and deliberate processes of a free society' which slow things down, allow for inconvenient questions to be raised and respect the dignity of all citizens, who are provided with opportunities to put forward their views: 21–22.

28 See H. Thompson, *Disorder: Hard Times in the 21st Century* (2022), 187; N. Machiavelli, *Discourses on Livy* (translated by J. Bondanella and P. Bondanella) ([1531], 1997).

29 Machiavelli, *Discourses*, 246, Book III, ch 1.

the world.[30] Liberal democracies need to be ready to hold course, and as necessary rebalance themselves, according to the basic principles which underpin them and give them life, when they are buffeted by the vicissitudes of politics. On the same theme, Jan-Werner Müller writes that there has to be a '*riduzione verso il principio*' for such a polity, to preserve its fundamental balance between a designated site for collectively binding decision-making involving the expression of political will through law-making and a protected place for 'the continuous formation of opinions and political judgments in society at large';[31] that is to say, to achieve a reasonably stable order which balances individual freedom and collective self-government.

A nation (or in the case of the UK, a group of nations) is in the final analysis constituted and rendered capable of functioning as a unit by loyalty to a collective ideal. The nation 'is an imagined political community', involving 'a deep, horizontal comradeship'.[32] If that dies, the nation will fall apart. One should not under-estimate the importance of the mythic or symbolic importance of a constitution in promoting loyalty to a collective identity, as the foundation for the state itself.[33] 'Freedom', 'the rule of law', 'responsible government' and 'democracy' constitute a focus for national loyalty with strong emotional resonance. The UK's constitution is a political achievement about which it is justified to feel a measure of pride. The executive, Parliament and the courts all have a part to play in sustaining that achievement into the future, and the forms of constitutional agency reposed in each of them should be exercised with that object in mind.

30 A. Vermeule, *Common Good Constitutionalism* (2022), 123–124, following John Henry Newman, *An Essay on the Development of Christian Doctrine* (2014): 'As circumstances change restlessly over time, principles must develop—in Newman's sense—precisely in order to retain their enduring, inherent shape'.

31 J-W. Müller, *Democracy Rules* (2021), 94.

32 B. Anderson, *Imagined Communities: Reflections on the Origin and Spread of Nationalism* (1983), 6–7.

33 Linda Colley gives an account of how Magna Carta, read as a charter of liberty and freedom, and genres of constitutional history which lauded those values used to serve this function for the UK: *The Gun, the Ship & the Pen: Warfare, Constitutions and the Making of the Modern World* (2021), 97–101, 217–218, 415–416.

Index

For the benefit of digital users, indexed terms that span two pages (e.g., 52–53) may, on occasion, appear on only one of those pages.

The manufacturer's authorised representative in the EU for product safety is Oxford University Press España S.A. of El Parque Empresarial San Fernando de Henares, Avenida de Castilla, 2 - 28830 Madrid (www.oup.es/en or product.safety@oup.com). OUP España S.A. also acts as importer into Spain of products made by the manufacturer.

Printed and bound by CPI Group (UK) Ltd, Croydon, CR0 4YY

17/09/2026

02218409-0002